the POWDER & the gLOry

the uLti... ...Ng

St. ...ry

the powder & the glory

the **ULTIMATE** GUIDE TO SNOWBOARDING

GREG DANIELLS

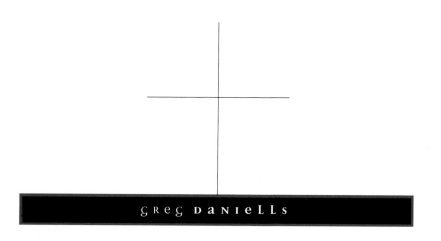

press
élan

a QUINTET BOOK

Published by élan press, an imprint of
General Publishing Co. Limited
30 Lesmill Road
Toronto, Canada M3B 2T6

Canadian Cataloguing in Publication Data is
available from the National Library of Canada.
Reprinted 1998
ISBN 1-55144-177-2

This book was designed and produced by
Quintet Publishing Limited,
6 Blundell Street, London N7 9BH

Creative Director: Richard Dewing
Art Director: Clare Reynolds
Designer: Grant Bowden at Deep
Editors: Catherine Burke, Keith Ryan
Photographer: Kurtis Croy
Illustrator: Simon Caulder

All photos by Kurtis Croy except:
AllSport: Mike Powell p. 6, 10 (*top*), 54, 88; Nathan
Bilow p. 22, 34, 46, and; Mike Cooper p. 115 (*top*)
Lori Hryhoruk: p. 5, 7 (*top*), 9, 33 (*bottom right*),
71 (*bottom*), 73, 80 (*bottom*), 115 (*bottom*)
Shaun W.-Smith: p. 40, 45, 62 (*top*), 74, 93 (*top*),
97 (*top*), 105 (*top*), 114, 118 (*top*), 124, 127
Eric Berger Photography: Eric Berger p. 8 (*bottom*), 119
Mountain Moments Photography: Greg Griffith p. 7
(*bottom*), 8 (*top, lower left and right*), 104, 118 (*bottom*)

BoarderCross ® (see Chapter 12) is a registered trademark.

Typeset in Great Britain by
Central Southern Typesetters, Eastbourne

Manufactured in Singapore by Eray Scan Pte. Ltd.

Printed in Singapore by Star Standard Industries Pte. Ltd.

**This book is dedicated to anyone who enjoys
the mountain playground.
It's all about having fun.**

contents

1

INtRODUCtION

S nowboarding is so much fun it should be illegal, hooking the imagination in an extreme and radical fashion, young or old. It's an exhilarating ride with an easy learning curve, which is why more and more people all over the planet are getting into the sport. For a skier, old terrain becomes a new playground. With a little knowledge and skill, you'll find snowboarding as natural as breathing fresh air and enjoying the scenery. That's what this book is about - setting you up and getting you excited about the sport. This book aims to get you off the couch and on the mountain, ready to ride. If you're a beginner, this book will take you through the basics, help you decide what equipment is best for you, teach you the moves you need to impress any die-hard boarder and even show you how to maintain your equipment, from filing to waxing. With some practice and a bit of commitment, you'll be up and boarding in no time – and probably never want to stop! This book is all about the coolest ride on the planet, pushing your limits and finding the snowboarder that lurks inside us all.

A very good place to begin is a ski resort that offers lessons in snowboarding. Here, you'll be able to put into practice what you learn through this book. First, you have to find the best resort for you, one that will have what you need to get you started. As more and more snowboarders head to the hills, more ski resorts are building snowparks and shaping their hills with the 'boarders desires in mind. What you're searching for in a great resort is a well-maintained snowpark with at least two pipes and halfpipes dug out, solid terrain changes in a run, such as steep roll-overs, compressions, banks, jumps, kickers, drops, and lots of long runs for good cruising.

As well as the changing terrain, a good resort will offer snowboard lessons from a snowboard instructor, not a ski instructor. They will ask you such questions as: What style of riding do you like? Can you ride fakie? Are you goofy? Do you want our snowboard park tour? Do you want an instructor in hard or soft boots? Your answers will help them determine what course to put you in. If you are asked whether you are confident on blue runs, you aren't dealing with a knowledgeable snowboard resort staff.

You'll be inspired by what you see on the mountain, by the riders and the maneuvers they can do. You'll soon be able to spot the appropriate terrain and snow conditions for your ability, and realize what it is you want to be able to do by what you see around you. The ne plus ultra mountain is the one that challenges you.

This type of resort exists all over the world. Resorts that host Snowboard World Cup events will have all you need. Here are just a few, in no particular order: Whistler, Canada. Innsbruck, Austria. Lake Louise, Canada. Leysin, Switzerland. Chamrousse, France. Val D'Isere, France. Oberstdorf, Germany. Madonna de Campiglio, Italy. Stratton, USA. Ichirino & Chugu, Japan. Sun Valley, USA. Mount Hood, USA. Naeba & Rusutsu, Japan.

If you seek endless vertical, your search ends with Whistler, Canada, which boasts two mile-high mountains, Blackcomb and Whistler, and one of the best snowboard parks in North America. The Whistler backcountry, whether you get there on your own or by helicopter, is full of untracked powder, glaciers, bowls, chutes and glades.

One of the best snowboard events is run at Stratton Mountain in Vermont, USA. The U.S. Open, the Big Kahuna of snowboarding events, has been held annually in Stratton since 1982 and features the Parallel Slalom, Big Air and Citizen Slingshot. Over the years it has attracted a virtual Who's Who of snowboarders: Tom Sims, Craig Kelly, Terry Kidwell, Shaun Palmer, Terje Haakonsen, and Martin Freinademetz to name a few.

If you ever reach the level of the extreme snowboarder, you'll want to visit Valdez, Alaska, where they now hold the King-of-The-Hill competition, formerly known as the World Snowboard Extreme Championships. Not for the novice, these events attract absolute adrenaline junkies who risk their lives to be crowned king. But that's a story for chapter 12.

the roots of the sport

In the beginning was the snurfer, a simple plywood board with non-skid pads for the feet and a rope with a handle attached to the nose, invented by an American named Sherman Poppens for his children. The first Snurfer competition was raced in Muskegon, Michigan, in 1968. It was a straight downhill speed race. A year later, Dimitrije Milovich, a surfer living in land-locked Utah, invented a molded polyester snowboard and christened it the "Winterstick." With a large spoon-shaped nose and both round and shallow tails, the Winterstick was the powder board. In 1978, Tom Sims produced his first prototype board in collaboration with Chuck Barfoot. The Sims board had a swallow tail similar to the Winterstick and was also a powder board. In 1983, Sims added steel edges to his board and won the first unofficial snowboard slalom event in Soda Springs, California.

In the early 1980s, ski resorts refused to allow these unusual riders on their slopes. Some would say snowboarders weren't allowed because they were riders with attitude, carving deep ruts through perfectly groomed slopes. Others maintain that the traditionalists couldn't understand that the youngsters were rebelling because snowboarding was as much fun as skiing.

Because of the resorts' snowboard ban, most of the research for board improvement was done in the backcountry on great powder. Hence, most of the early boards were simply powder boards. However, that did not stop innovators like Terry Kidwell from removing the Winterstick's metal fin to perform basic freestyle tricks in 1980.

While Kidwell began North America's domination of freestyle, the Europeans honed their skills and designs on alpine racing. José Fernanades, a Swiss skateboarding champion, created the plate binding for snowboard racing in the early eighties. With extreme binding angles and narrow race boards, Euro-carving was born. In 1987, the first official World Championships were organized in Brechenridge, Colorado, USA, and in St-Moritz-Livigno, Switzerland. As you can imagine, North Americans won the freestyle events and the Europeans won the alpine racing.

The entrepreneur and inventor who brought the sport into the public conscience was Jake Burton Carpenter. He not only refined the snurfer, he acted as the sport's ambassador to the ski industry and won boarders the right to ride. There are many designers, manufacturers and riders who have contributed to and shaped the equipment and riding styles we enjoy today, and there will be many more. The sport is young and riders are constantly challenging the industry to respond. Started by surfers and influenced by skiers and skateboarders, snowboarding is now enjoyed by people all over the world and its notoriety has earned it a place at the 1998 Winter Olympics in Nagano, Japan.

DON't **miss** the **ride**. get **ON BOARD**

everything you
always wanted to know about
SNOWBOARDING but were afraid to ask

k nowing your equipment makes learning any sport easier and helps you understand your ability and your level of competence. With the different styles of boarding, from freestyle to racing, and the endless tricks and moves to perform, from boning out a method to carving 360s, understanding snowboard equipment will help you decide what style is for you, what snow conditions to avoid and why you may not be improving as quickly as you would like.

SNOWBOARD anatomy: the BASICS

nose - The front tip of the board. Turned up slightly, the nose is needed to help the board slide on snow more efficiently. Without a nose your board would dive into powder.

waist - The narrowest part of the board.

tail - The back tip of the board, behind the back foot. If you have a twin tip board, the nose and tail will look the same.

SNOWBOARD **anatomy**: the BASICS

e D G e S - All modern snowboards have metal edges that allow you to steer your board and control your speed, especially on hard or icy surfaces. There are two types of edges: solid and cracked. A solid edge is continuous, wrapping around the entire board for added strength. The cracked edge is intentionally cracked in very small sections to offer more flexibility.

B I N D I N G S - Bindings are attached to the board with screws, and provide the interface between the boot and board. Now, there is more than one way to buckle in your boot, but back in the sport's infancy, bindings were just loose straps or a rope with a handle attached to the board's nose. The invention of the now common high back binding for freeride boots was one of the most important moments in snowboard history. The high back binding provides support and control, and allows snowboarders to go beyond mere surfing.

B a s e - The running surface of your board. Your base dictates how effortlessly you glide over the snow. The base material is polyethylene, commonly referred to as P TEX. A number of different bases exist to meet the demands of different skill levels and snow conditions. The inexpensive extruded base is used on low-end to intermediate boards. A sintered base is made with a higher quality polyethylene, and holds the wax longer. The electra base, which takes on a black color due to the carbon and graphite added to the polyethylene, is advantageous in warmer, wet snow conditions.

S I D e w a L L - This holds the board together, protecting the side and the material inside the board.

L e a S H - A safety device attached to the front binding and secured to your front leg when riding. A leash can also help solve the problem of a runaway board when getting in or out of your bindings. If you attach the leash around the back binding it can be used as a carrying strap.

s t o m p p a d - Found between the two bindings, the stomp pad is a resting place for your back foot when out of its bindings.

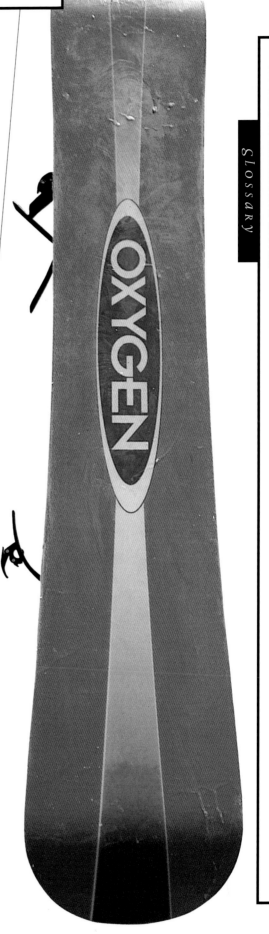

OXYGEN

and for the
technically-minded...

nose and tail radius

This is the shape of the nose and tail of the board. The radius of the nose and tail influences turning, flotation, swing weight, and effective edge. The radius varies depending on the board's purpose of design.

effective edge (running length)

Determined by how much of the board's edge meets the snow when turning. The length of your board is not the same thing as its effective edge.

A continuous edge does wrap around the entire board, but the turned up portion of the nose and tail will not touch the snow during a turn and, are not part of your effective edge.

sidecut

The difference in width between the nose, waist and tail. If you put your snowboard on the ground and look at its shape you will see the subtle differences in the sidecut. When a snowboard is put on edge it will create an arc in the snow. Different board types have different sidecuts. For example, a Giant Slalom board will create a larger arc in the snow, but will be slower edge-to-edge. A Slalom board will have a deeper (narrower) sidecut with a quicker edge-to-edge, but will be less stable at high speeds. Try to put your board on edge and carve a full 360 degree circle turn. What is the radius of that circle? The sidecut is related to the size of that circle.

nose, waist, and tail widths

The nose, waist, and tail widths effect the ride you will experience. The waist width is the narrowest part of the board, and can be in the center of the board or back of center. The width of the nose and tail can be the same, as in a twin tip board, or different, as in a directional board.

weight

Everything on your board contributes to its overall weight, such as the bindings, screws, leash, and stomp pad. The trend is definitely moving to lighter boards. The only thing to be careful about is the durability of the product. Do not compromise durability for lightness.

fLex

The stiffness or softness of your board. The amount of flex in your board will be related to your body weight and desired riding style. A freestyle board generally has a very soft flex. With a soft flex most of your weight will be in the middle of the board. This board will feel shorter and easier to turn, but less stable at high speeds. A race board usually has a very stiff flex, and your weight and pressure are distributed along the entire edge. This provides stability, but less maneuverability.

camBeR

Camber is the arch in your board. This arch provides a rebound or energy release out of your turns. A brand new board feels snappy and responsive. The board reacts to the pressure you apply. When the camber breaks down, your board's response will be slow. I refer to this as a "dead" board. Camber also relates to your body weight. Your weight will influences the camber and how it distributes your weight.

SWING WeIGHt

The ease with which the board swings is proportional to the swing weight or length of the board. For shorter, zippy swings or spins use a shorter board. Your maneuverability increases with a reduced swing weight. Your stability increases with greater swing weight or a longer board.

tORSIONaL stiffNess

Torsional stiffness refers to how much your snowboard resists twisting or bending. Stand on your board, strapped in, and try to flex the board heel to toe with your feet. You can see that your board not only flexes from nose to tail, but from heel edge to toe edge. When you turn and put the board on edge, only the widest parts of your board (nose and tail) will meet the snow first. The more torsionally stiff your board is the less chance it will chatter out, and the more stable it will be at high speeds. A freestyle board is torsionally soft, making it turn easier at slower speeds. Racing or alpine boards are torsionally very stiff, providing stability when carving at high speeds.

INSeRtS

Small threaded holes for the bolts used to mount the bindings. Inserts allow for a wide variety of stance options.

gLOSSaRy

Camber: Camber is the arch in your board. / **Effective Edge:** The running length of your board. / **Flex:** The stiffness or softness of your board. / **Inserts:** These are small threaded holes in the board for the bolts used to mount the bindings. / **Nose and Tail radius:** This is the shape of the nose and tail of the board. / **Sidecut:** The difference in width between the nose, waist and tail. / **Swing Weight:** The ease with which the board swings is proportional to the swing weight or length of the board. / **Torsional stiffness:** Torsional stiffness refers to how much your snowboard resists twisting or bending when you put it on edge and apply pressure to it.

are aLL boards the same?

Absolutely not! With one quick look at a ski area or snowboard magazine you will see a wide variety of snowboards. As in any sport, there is a variety of equipment to suit different sizes, abilities, styles, and trends. The snowboarding industry has responded with several boards to choose from. Before buying a board, however, you should ask yourself a few questions.

- How tall are you? How much do you weigh? Your equipment should be proportionate to your height and weight, similar to mountain biking or golfing.
- What kind of riding interests you the most? Freestyle, freeride, freecarve, or alpine. Specific boards are used for specific styles.
- What is your local hill like? Consider the terrain, the typical local snow conditions, and the vertical drop.

Board design is always evolving and the result is a different board for everyone, including your dog. Several things will influence the design of snowboards, such as trends, customer demands, media, R&D, demographics, etc. Boards will differ in flex, shape, construction, graphics and size.

There are boards made for very specialized types of riding while others are designed to be more versatile. It is important to note that the more specialized your equipment, the less versatile it will be, and vice versa.

The most popular snowboarding activities fall into four categories: one, halfpipe and freestyle; two, freeride; three, freecarve; and four, race.

halfpipe and freestyle

Freestyle boards are designed for the halfpipe, the snowboard park or milking the mountain for hits. This snowboarder is on a seek-and-destroy mission to hit a multitude of jumps, perform stupendous spinning tricks, and ride fakie as much as possible. Freestyle riders also ride in groups and move from jump-to-jump together, for whatever reason. It can be a social experience or just constant one-upmanship.

With a small nose and tail, these short, wide boards have less swing weight, making the board easier to spin and more maneuverable in the snow and air. The flex is consistent and the stance centered. Freestyle boards have twin tips – identical nose and tail widths – that help when riding fakie (backwards). These boards account for the majority of retail sales. Freestyle boards are usually ridden with soft boots, and are not suited for deep powder, freeriding, or performance on icy conditions.

Freestyle should never be pinned down as one or two things – it shall remain open in my book. Freestyle snowboarding will continue to progress and evolve in its own unique way.

freeride

This rider rides the entire mountain from top to bottom and only cares about getting as much powder as possible. Since they ride a variety of terrain, they demand more from their equipment. Usually ridden with soft boots, these boards have deeper sidecuts for quick turning, and extra length for stability at higher speeds. They are directional boards, i.e. they have a definite nose and tail, and the stance and flex pattern is set slightly back from the center.

freecarve (alpine)

A new breed of alpinists, the freecarver wants both performance and versatility when riding off-piste (off the groomed runs). Freecarve boards borrow the best from the freeride and race boards. They perform very well on groomed and hard packed snow, but can also be ridden off-piste or on powder, through the trees, and on bumpy terrain. The design features a wider board with a longer nose and tail to help planing in powder. Typically, they have a softer flex in the nose than in the tail for better riding in off-piste and all mountain terrain. Usually ridden with hard shell boots, they are torsionally stiff to keep the board stable at high speeds. Not all freecarve boards can be ridden fakie, but most can be as there is a small but somewhat functional tail.

race

The racer is a rare breed in the snowboarding world. Similar to the ski racer, the snowboard racer seeks minimum movement for maximum reaction, always pushing the limits of speed. Some expert freecarvers cross over to this speed mission. Race boards do not have to be ridden by racers, but they represent a very serious carver interested in maximum performance, trying to defy gravity with the help of technology, the fall line and natural speed. Every technical detail in racing makes a significant difference to performance and speed.

The boards are long and skinny with a small nose and zero tail to maximize edge contact. They are very specialized for hard pack icy conditions, and do not fair well off groomed runs. Commonly used with very stiff boots, most race boards are symmetrical, with only slalom boards using an asymmetrical shape.

Level of ability is everything. The better the rider's ability and performance, the stiffer the equipment.

specific equipment for women

Most companies have realized that the average size and shape of women differs from that of men, and that this affects how the board performs. Therefore, boards have been designed for, and marketed to, women, based on average sizes and weights. These boards are narrower, due to smaller feet, and have a softer flex, due to lighter weight. A guy with the same foot size and weight could ride them, but most would give them thumbs down to protect their cool image and masculinity. Of course, these boards are marketed to women with signature models, different graphics, and advertising. The most important thing to understand is that, similar to men, women vary in size and may or may not be ideally suited for these "small, gumby flexed boards."

BINDING, Cants & INSERTS

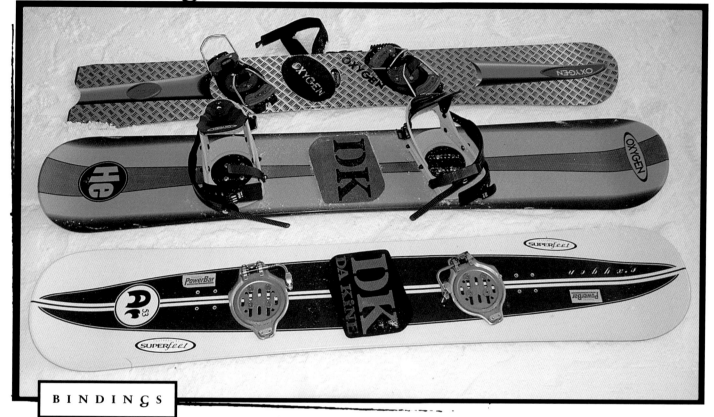

BINDINGS

There are three types of bindings – plate, freestyle, and step-in. Bindings will vary slightly from one manufacturer to another, but all try to find common ground between the boot and binding interface. The better the boot and binding work together, the more control the rider has. Snowboard bindings do not release and never will – releasable binding would be too dangerous. With skis, your individual body parts can move on their own whether you want them to or not. Even at slow speeds, one ski can go one way while the other ski goes another, and your knee or ankle has no choice but to twist. In snowboarding, your entire body twists with the turn, not just your individual body parts.

Plate

Plate binding is made for hard shell boots only. There is very little play in the binding, allowing for a quick edge-to-edge response. The boot and binding become one. This type of binding is very easy to get in and out of. Some plate bindings have a slight lateral flex. Most plate bindings come canted (small bevelled edges under the boot which force the foot to lean), but the trend is moving toward a flat binding with no canting.

Glossary

Cants: Small bevelled edges under the boot which force the foot to lean. / **Freecarve:** The freecarver wants both performance and versatility. / **Off piste:** Anywhere off the groomed runs. / **Plate binding:** Made for hard shell boots only. There is very little play in the binding, allowing for a quick edge-to-edge response. / **Race:** The snowboard racer seeks minimum movement for maximum reaction, always pushing the limits of speed.

This style of binding has been the most popular or most common over the years. This binding is used only with soft boots and usually has two straps; one covering the toe area, and the other, over the top of the foot. These bindings are very versatile for freestyle and freeriding. There are some companies who make a three-strap freeride binding. The idea is that the binding offers more support and a quicker edge-to-edge response. Fine for all mountain freeriding, the three-strap design is too restrictive for freestyle riding.

the HIGH BACK AND FORWARD Lean

When snowboards were first built (pre-high back era), it was the bindings, or rather the lack of bindings, that held us back in terms of control. Since there was no support, you could not put the board on edge as needed, especially heelside. The invention of the high back is one of the more significant developments in snowboarding equipment. It allowed the rider to progress rapidly and rip it up on the hard pack, which is not possible with Velcro straps or bungy cords. With an adjustable forward lean, the board reacts quicker when your calf or ankle leans back against it. On your toe edge, you can use your knees, ankles, and hips to bend and lean into the hill. On your heel side, your ankles do not bend backwards; therefore, you have one less joint to use. This means you must really take advantage of the forward lean option to allow for the board to be tipped on edge without straightening the legs.

It seems ironic and moronic that, after developing and promoting all these performance enhancers in equipment, the snowboard industry has taken a step backwards by promoting low back binding. You might as well be riding as they did fifteen years ago, with little to no control. There is no advantage to using a low back binding. The argument that they are better for freestyle maneuvers is bogus. Top pro freestylers would never use them. Trends come and go and the public is always a few years behind. The same thing happened with the wide stances and baggy pants. People learned the hard way that it didn't work. I predict the same thing will happen with low backs. As companies and riders realize there is no advantage, they will be phased out.

step-in BINDINGS

The step-in binding system is definitely one of the most exciting new trends in snowboard equipment today. K2 Snowboards lead the way with the first step-in system, compatible with their own boots. This combines the best of both hard and soft boots to produce a fantastic all-mountain freeriding boot binding. This system is also easy to get in and out of. The trend is catching on as other companies are trying to develop their own versions. Each company only works with their boot, which means the boards and boots from separate companies are not interchangeable. Only time will tell but the step-in system may be the future. There are also step-in systems made for hard shell boots. Look for a boot with adjustable "forward lean" – as you can imagine, once you take away the binding, the boot must have the appropriate amount of forward lean or it will be equivalent to riding low back bindings. Each step-in system may be slightly different, so take the time to read the manual and understand fully how they work before getting out there on the snow.

Glossary

Freestyle/Freeride: Used only with soft boots and usually has two straps, very versatile for freestyle and freeriding. / **Step-in Bindings:** Combines the best of both hard and soft boots to produce a fantastic all-mountain freeriding boot binding.

cants

Cants are small bevelled plates that provide a lean or a tilt under the binding. In snowboarding, these are used to tilt the feet inwards. Cants were very popular at one time, but now are more or less out. Back in the early freestyle days, the idea was to get the knees together. The cants brought the knees very close together and forced the rider over the middle of the board. But what we discovered, through trial and error, is that having your knees together balanced you on a triangle, an unstable platform. Since your knees were locked, you could not bend to absorb pressures building up on the board, or control your edge pressure properly. Cants also brought the back knee into the front knee, resulting in

an off-centered rider. The result was too much weight over the front foot, causing the tail to skid around or wash out, and less board performance as the weight was not centered over the board's camber or flex point. Plate bindings are still made with canting built in, but world cup riders are riding their bindings flat.

One of the main reasons for driving the knees together was for a lower center of mass, but the same effect can be achieved by just bending your knees more. You can then control your edge power and shock absorption with a wider and more stable stance.

setting it up

regular

goofy

are you regular or goofy?

Put your best foot forward and go from there. Approximately 75% of the world's snowboarders are "regular" footed. This means they ride with their left foot forward. The other 25% are sometimes referred to as "goofy" footed, riding with their right foot forward.

There is no advantage to riding goofy or regular. Do what comes naturally. If you have done related board sports, such as skateboarding, surfing, skim boarding, wind surfing,

slalom water skiing, or wakeboarding, then your footing will be the same. If you have never done any of these sports, try these exercises to determine your forward foot:

- If you were to run and slide on a slippery surface, which foot would you put forward?
- Play around on a skateboard. You don't have to even really move on it, but try to feel out which way or which foot would go forward naturally.

stance width

Unlike skiing where your feet can move freely, a snowboarder's base of support (BOS) is a fixed position. An appropriate stance width (the distance between your feet) allows for independent leg action and keeps the body structurally aligned, which promotes good balance. Your stance width is influenced by your height, weight, and leg length. If your BOS is too narrow you will loose balance and stability. A good example of this is the mono skier.

Imagine if your feet were two inches apart - you would fall over all the time. So you need to widen your stance to provide a natural, balanced position. If you stand too wide, your board performance will suffer. Regardless your preferred riding style, standing with your feet approximately shoulder width apart is an excellent place to start. Your stance width determines how balanced you will be on your board.

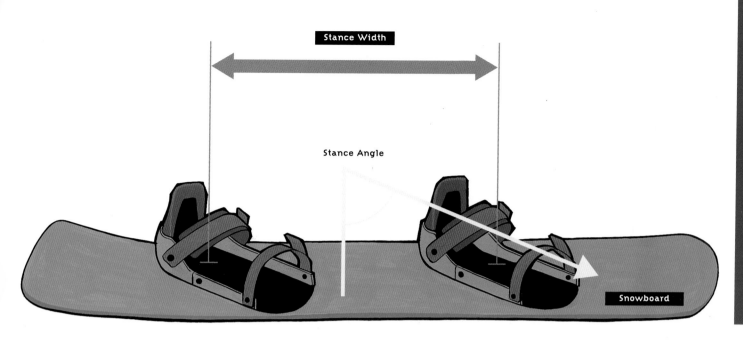

Stance Width

Stance Angle

Snowboard

stance angles

Due to binding placement, riding style and snow conditions, stance angles vary from snowboarder to snowboarder. For example, if you ride a freestyle board, then your stance angle will be square and centered on the board. If you ride an alpine or freeride board, your stance angle will be forward. You have to decide yourself what is the best angle. Change your stance angles when the snow conditions change from icy to powder, when you're carving the mountain or when you're just riding for hits.

glossary

Binding Positioning: You can adjust your bindings to match your riding style and daily snow conditions. / **Goofy footed:** Riding with your right foot forward. / **Regular footed:** Riding with your left foot forward. / **Stance Angles:** Due to binding placement, riding style and snow conditions, stance angles vary from snowboarder to snowboarder. / **Stance width:** The distance between your feet.

BINDING POSITIONING

As with stance angle, you can adjust your bindings to match your riding style and daily snow conditions. You can increase the forward lean on your high backs to improve your heelside turns. You can adjust straps to hold your foot snugly and create more stability between you and your board.

You can customize your board for a better ride by changing your stance width, your stance angle, your bindings, or by adding cants. Who you are and what you are doing dictate all of the above. Experiment. Bring a small screwdriver with you when you ride and adjust your board whenever you feel it necessary.

tips for better boarding

- Since snowboarding is a dynamic sport, clothes should be functional and practical for the winter mountain environment. Snow and weather conditions can change quickly and your clothes must keep you warm and dry. If you underdress you could be in trouble. If you come in your Elvis outfit you may have a negative experience.
- Before going out, layer your clothes: long underwear, shirt, sweater, fleece, and then a jacket. Don't underestimate long underwear. It keeps your body warm in all weather conditions. Be aware of the conditions in your local area. For example, the west coast of North America is warm and gets a lot of rain so waterproof outerwear is critical. For those in the east, the temperatures are very cold and dry so deal with it accordingly. Other clothing you should have: gloves, mitts, and hats.

3

get on board
first moves

Okay, now that you have some techno-knowledge, it's time to strap on your board and take it out for a test drive. Make it easy on yourself – pick a bright sunny day, an easy slope with soft powder and a great snowboard instructor. As you experience the sensation of the board on the snow – trying to control your speed and destination – don't be surprised if you fall more than once. It's all part of the learning curve: within a couple of days or even hours, you'll be moving on to more challenging levels. However, it is important to learn how to fall and get back up to minimize injury. With the understanding of basic snowboard skills, you will decrease the odds of falling, increase your comfort level and begin to excel at the sport.

warm up exercises and stretching

To reduce injury and improve your ride, try a number of warm up exercises and a stretching routine. Warm up by running on the spot, stride jumps, or taking a long swift walk from the parking lot. Stretch out the muscle groups in your upper and lower body, focusing on your legs, hamstrings, calves, hips, and gluteus. You'll be using these muscle groups the most while snowboarding. Once you feel warm and loose, buckle yourself into your boots and strap on your board.

strapping in, buckling up - equipment

All bindings – freestyle, plate, or step-ins – have different strap-in procedures. When you purchase your bindings, read all the print material associated with them. There are, however, two cardinal rules that apply to all three bindings. First, remove all snow from your bindings and the bottom of your boots. Second, and this is essential, always strap in your front boot first.

freestyle bindings/soft boots

Freestyle and freeride bindings are the most popular set up. Follow these steps and you're in:

• Place your boot to the back of the binding, against the high back.
• Fasten the top strap first to keep your boot in place.
• Then, fasten the toe strap.

If you have a third strap around the ankle (as in the Burton Flex binding, for example), fasten this strap last. The fit should be snug so that your boot does not lift up in the binding. You don't want any play in the heel. To release your boot, undo the ratchets, bails, or clips, and step out.

plate BINDINGS/HARD BOOTS

Plate bindings are easier and faster to get in and out of. Place your heel in first, lower the boot into the binding, then snap the toe bail onto the boot. The toe bail should fit tightly and snap down with tension. If the snap is not easy and smooth, check your heel and make sure it is in the binding properly. If you're still not happy with the fit, do yourself a favor and get the binding adjusted by a professional. To release the boot from the bindings, snap up the toe bail and lift your boot out.

step-IN BINDINGS

This could be the future! Only time will tell, but everyone seems to be pretty stoked on the step-in system. There are a number of versions of the step-in binding on the market designed for both hard and soft shell boots. Very similar to a clip-less pedal on a bike shoe, the system is self-explanatory. Just line the boot up with the binding and step in. Apply your weight and your boot will click into place. To get out, pull on the cord or tab and step out. Read the print material that comes with the binding so you are familiar with how to step in and out properly.

BOARD famILIaRIZatION exercises

Do these exercises with the front foot strapped into the bindings and the back foot free:

exercise ONe

Feel the weight of the board by standing on your free foot and lifting the board up. Do this a number of times so you can get a sense of the board's dimensions and what you're strapped to.

exercise two

Feel how the board slides across the snow by trying a static pivot.

Put your weight on your free foot, and, using your strapped-in foot, move the board's tail back and forth.

exercise three

To understand how the board travels and your body with it, pivot the board around your free foot. Put your weight on your free foot, slide your board on the snow and move your body in the direction of travel. Keep the board slightly on edge to help you complete the pivot.

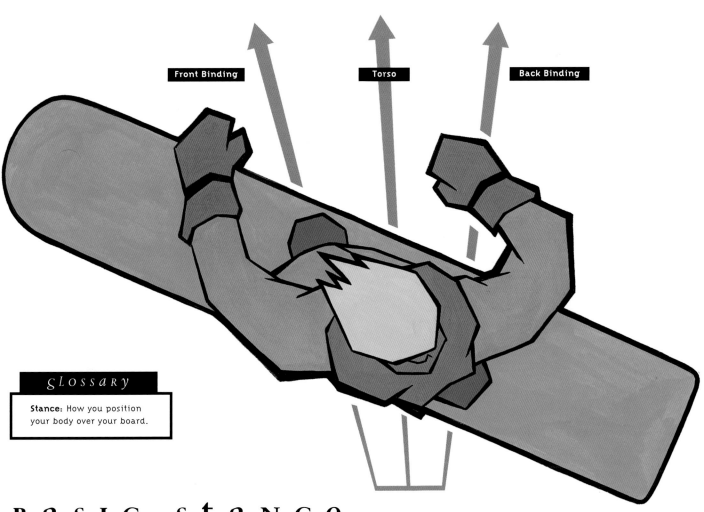

Front Binding

Torso

Back Binding

Glossary

Stance: How you position your body over your board.

Basic Stance

ankles, knees, hips, torso, arms, head and eyes

Your basic stance – how you position your body over your board – relates directly to your balance. For the basics, keep your torso tall and upright, your ankles and knees flexed, your arms out and loose for maintaining balance over the board, and remember to always look where you want to go. When you have your back foot out of the binding, it is important to keep your weight centered over the front foot. Since your front foot is your base of support, this will be one of the only times when your weight is centered over the front foot. Adapt your balance. For more on stance, refer to Snowboard Skills later on in this chapter.

faLLINg over aNd gettINg up

When first learning a sport, it is inevitable that you will fall. These tips will help you lessen the impact and recover quickly. When you catch an edge in the snow, you will lose your balance and fall. Sometimes this happens faster than you can react. When you fall toe side or forward, spread the impact out by sliding or rolling.

If you fall heel side or backwards, roll onto your back, tuck your chin into your chest, and keep your hands under your knees. If you keep your speed to a minimum, when you catch an edge and lose your balance, you will just fall over. Practice falling on the flats. You might want to invest in safety pads such as wrist guards or knee pads.

Getting up off your heel side after you've fallen backwards can be tricky. First, get your weight over the board. Use your back hand to push off the snow, bend your knees and ankles, and move your body over the bindings. Once your center of mass is over the board and bindings, stand up.

Getting up off the toe side after a forward fall is easy. Bend your knees and ankles, move your center of mass over the board, push off the snow with your hands and stand up. Make sure the board is perpendicular to the fall line (the imaginary path a ball would follow if rolled down a hill) before you stand up, otherwise you'll start moving down the slope before you're balanced.

3

4

5

turning over onto your toe edge

2

It is important to learn how to get up from a sitting position and when you want to change edges without turning. The easiest way to get to your feet is from your toe edge. Lie on your back, bend your knees into your chest, put the tail of your board into the snow, roll the nose and yourself over until you are facing the snow on the toe edge and stand up. For an easier roll, angle the board's tail slightly downhill. Keep your upper and lower body together as you roll. Again, make sure your board is perpendicular to the fall line before standing up.

6

1

glossary

Fall Line: The imaginary path a ball would follow if rolled down a hill.
Flats: The level portion of a hill or mountain (no incline).

7

You need to know how to skate on your board to traverse the flat, move along in lift lines, and get on and off the chair. With your front foot as your base of support, your free back foot propels you along the flat. This movement is similar to what you do when you are skateboarding. You can push with your free foot from either the toe side or the heel side. Keep your weight over the front foot, look where you want to go, and take comfortable strides. Feel the board slide over the snow, and always feel for control. To feel that control, go as slow as you have to. Use the edge of the board to help you keep your balance. As you become more comfortable with your balance and equipment, skating becomes easy and natural.

If you have to skate across a slight pitch or incline, keep your free foot on the uphill edge in front of the board regardless of toe or heel edge and use your board's edge to maintain balance.

MOVING UP THE SLOPE

Your upper body should face the direction of travel, which is now uphill. Keep your board perpendicular to the fall line, dig the toe side edge into the snow, take a big step with your free foot in front of your board, and a little step with the board behind. Make sure to lift your board completely off the snow, be aggressive and stay balanced.

Glossary

Skate: Pulling your board across a flat using a motion similar to ice skating.

SNOWBOARD SKILLS

To truly understand and analyze snowboarding (from beginner to expert riding), it is important to have a good understanding of snowboard skills. If you do, this will provide a solid foundation that will enable you to get the most out of both this book and your snowboarding. It is important to note that it takes much mileage to master all the skills and blend them, but it is a good place to start, an organized approach if you will, and it will also allow you to analyze your own riding. It takes years to become an expert, but you'll have an authentically awesome time getting there.

stance and Balance

Being balanced at all times is the cornerstone to expert snowboarding. How you stand over your board will greatly influence your balance. Think of your body as a skeletal structure. You are balanced when you are structurally aligned over your feet. All joints should be slightly flexed and ready for movement. Your upper body should remain tall and in line with your feet. Keep your hands at a comfortable level and use them to aid balance.

your center of mass (com)

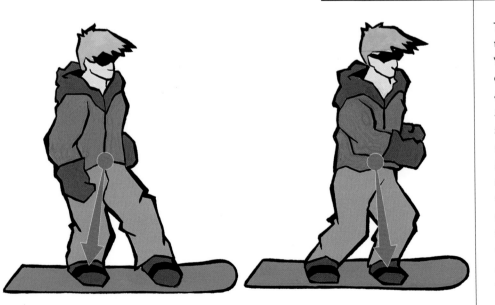

Think of it as just inside your navel – must be balanced over your board. Your base of support (BOS), which is essentially your feet, should always allow your center of mass to be as balanced as possible. If your base of support (stance width) is too narrow, or wide, you will not be in the optimum balance position. Different snowboard disciplines will dictate your stance width. For example, alpine requires a narrower stance width and freestyle wider, but it is important to understand the relationship between COM, BOS, and general stance and balance principles (see diagram).

While your stance width is influenced by the length of your leg, your stance angles will depend on your style of riding (alpine, freestyle, or freeride). As a rule, you should always be in line with your feet, but sometimes adjustments are needed. The more you are in the fall line, the more your angles will be forward, allowing you to be more in line with your direction of travel when riding. If you like to ride the pipe and park, your stance will be straight across the board because you are riding a transition sideways, or hitting a jump standing sideways. A freerider will have something between these two stances. If you are riding a square stance, but come to a mogul run, you will have to adjust your body to be a little more in the fall line. In deep powder, you may want to sit back a bit, or move your stance back of center. Stance will vary from snowboarder to snowboarder. Different things influence stance, such as personal preference, experience, trends, goals, style of riding, etc. Regardless how your bindings are set up, the most important thing is to be centered over your feet.

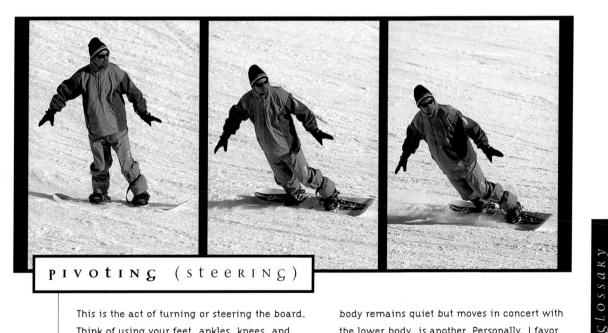

PIVOTING (STEERING)

This is the act of turning or steering the board. Think of using your feet, ankles, knees, and hips as tools to steer the board. There are two different techniques to turn the board. Rotation, or what some call anticipation, using the upper body to help lead into or initiate a turn, is one way. Counter rotation, when the lower body steers while the upper body remains quiet but moves in concert with the lower body, is another. Personally, I favor counter rotation as it promotes minimum movement for the maximum reaction. If you can control the board with the lower body, you will be much better off. Using the upper body to turn, I feel, can lead to bad boarding habits.

GLOSSARY

Balance: Think of your body as a skeletal structure. You are balanced when you are structurally aligned over your feet. / **Base of support (BOS):** Essentially, your feet. / **Center of mass (COM):** Think of it as just inside your navel. / **Edging:** The act of putting the board "on edge." / **Pivoting:** The act of turning or steering the board. / **Rotation:** The act of turning or steering the board (alpine, freestyle, or freeride) / **Stance angles:** Depend on your style of riding (alpine, freestyle, or freeride) / **Stance width:** The distance between your feet when boarding.

Heel Edge **Toe Edge**

EDGING

This is the act of putting the board "on edge." To use edges, an edge angle must be created. This is the angle created between the raised edge of your board and the snow. How much or how little edge you use will depend on a variety of factors, but developing the edging skill is critical for intermediate to advanced snowboarding (see diagram).

When using your board's edges, it is important to understand the relationship between angulation and inclination. Angulation is created by the lower body, i.e. hips, knees, and ankles, compensating for large edge angles by keeping the upper body balanced over the board's edge.

Inclination or banking happens as you lean into your turn. You probably know the feeling already. It's similar to leaning into a turn on a mountain bike or motorcycle. Inclining is a natural thing to do and feels great, but too much can cause you to loose your balance. If you incline too much in relation to the edge angle without using appropriate angulation to compensate, you will loose your balance.

As you start to link turns, your speed will increase, producing pressure on your board and body. Pressure affects snowboarding in two ways: when your base is flat and when you're on an edge. Overall pressure is a combination of edge and flat base pressures. To deal with these pressures, it is important to start flexing in the knees and ankles.

There are two ways to pressure the board. "Up-unweighting," a vertical move, is when you extend through your knees and ankles to "unweight" the board of pressure. "Down-unweighting" means you flex your knees and ankles and extend the legs out to the side, a lateral move. Moguls require down-unweighting and an extension out to the side (see diagram).

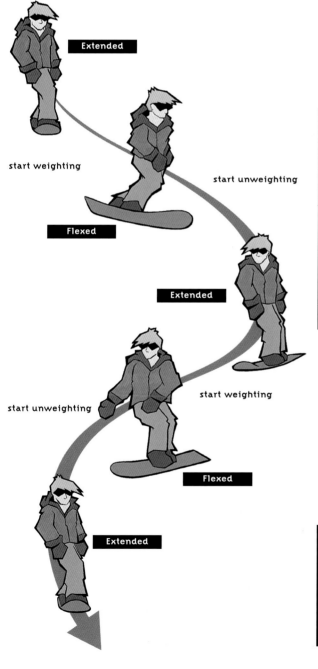

t i m i n g and c o o r d i n a t i o n

Timing and coordination is a blending of all the above skills. A true expert will be able to harmonize all movements at the right time, and, consequently, will look perfect always. These riders are a pleasure to watch. Every movement will happen at the right time and in sync with each other.

g l o s s a r y

Angulation: Created by the lower body, i.e. hips, knees, and ankles, compensating for large edge angles by keeping the upper body balanced over the board's edge. / **Down-unweighting:** Flexing your knees and ankles and extend the legs out to the side, a lateral move. / **Inclination:** Inclination or banking happens as you lean into your turn. / **Pressure:** As you start to link turns, your speed will increase, producing pressure on your board and body. / **Up-unweighting:** A vertical move in which you extend through your knees and ankles to "unweight" the board of pressure.

4

MOVING DOWNHILL

N ow that you understand your equipment, how to stand on it and move on the flat, fall and get back up, your next challange is to control your speed and stop at will. If you have an understanding of the basic snowboard skills – stance and balance, pivoting, edging and pressure – you will find it easy to slow down, pick up speed and stop. A number of easy exercises follow to help you move on to the next level in chapter 5, where you'll learn about using lifts, and the one you've being waiting for, Chapter 6: Basic Turns. Be certain you understand your speed and stopping skills before you attempt crashing off a chair lift or springing through the trees. For these exercises, try a moderate green (beginner's) run with a fall line pitch.

re-mounting on a gradient

Remember, before you can go downhill, you have to stand up on your board. Since this is your very first time moving downhill, keep your board across the hill and perpendicular to the fall line before you stand up, regardless of heel or toe edge. This may seem obvious now, but on the hill many forget and stand up with

their boards in the fall line and before they realize what's happening, they're moving down the hill backwards. Once standing, keep an equal amount of edge pressure on the board to ensure that you don't start moving before you are ready. You should find it easier to stand up from a gradient than from a flat.

SIDesLIPPING

SIDesLIPPING - toe edge

This exercise will help you learn how to stop, and how to control your speed. When sideslipping you do not have to start on your toe side. Start on whatever edge feels more comfortable. If you do find yourself on your toe side, however, here's what to do:

Since you are strapped into both bindings, facing up the hill and moving, the first thing to do is take it easy. Maintain good stance and balance. Keep equal pressure on both feet. By using your knees and ankles you can play with the edge angle. Decrease the amount of edge angle (the angle between the base of your board and the

snow) and you will start to move down the hill; increase the edge angle and you will slow down. I think of this as the gas pedal. Resist the urge to turn around and look down the hill. Stay loose and relaxed. Try not to rock the edge.

traverse SIDesLip to a sLow stop

With this exercise you will travel farther and faster across the hill than you did with the 'Falling Leaf' sideslip. The traverse gives you the feeling of moving on the snow, and you experience your first sensation of snowboarding! Keep in mind, since you are covering more of the run, pay attention to other snowboards and ski traffic, take your time and enjoy yourself.

If you are on your toe edge, apply slightly more pressure to the front toe and slide across the hill. If you are on your heel edge, apply the same pressure to the front heel. Go slow. Stay balanced and focus. Be careful not to apply too much pressure to your front foot, and keep consistent pressure on the entire edge, so that the board is always sliding. Do not use too much edge. Keep the board flat and slide.

To stop, apply equal pressure to both feet and increase the amount of edge angle. This will skid the board and help you come to a slow, controlled stop.

Since you can't turn yet, roll over to change direction. Sit down, roll over and stand up, then apply slightly more pressure to the front foot on the other edge. Keep a centered stance. Look in the direction of travel, and don't move your body around. As you gain confidence, flirt with speed and the fall line.

tips for better boarding

These basic sideslip traverses will help you learn how to maintain your balance, stop, control direction, and, to a certain extent, control speed. It is also the first time you will be sliding down the hill, so be comfortable with each step before moving onto the next.

SIDESLIPPING

- If you fall, place your board across the fall line before you attempt to get up.
- While standing, maintain equal pressure on both feet to avoid rocking the edge and falling.
- Keep your eyes focused on the direction you are traveling, not down at the snow.
- Keep your body upright, arms out for balance, knees and ankles flexed.
- To control speed, slide the board more and equalize the pressure.

FALLING LEAF

- Only a slight pressure change from one foot to the other is needed to change direction.
- Shift your pressure not your body position.

TRAVERSE

- Control your speed. Go slow.
- Keep a centered stance and look in the direction of travel. Don't twist your upper body.
- Only a slight amount of pressure in the front foot is needed to get moving. Deep angle edges can land you in the snow.

STANCE/BALANCE PROBLEMS

- Don't bend at the waist. Keep a tall upper body with flexed knees and ankles. Keep hands in a quiet, ready position.

5

UPWARDLy moBILe
USING Lifts

fifteen years ago, snowboarders were forbidden to ride the ski lifts at ski resorts. Now, however, the lifts have never been better, and snowboarders deserve every bit of it because we have brought much needed revenue to the hills. Kids are more enthusiastic then ever about this winter sport and the beautiful thing is, they will grow up never knowing that lift discrimination ever existed. Of the various types of ski lifts around the world, I will discuss the more common ones you will experience on the hill (surface or tow lifts and chair lifts), how to get on and off them, and how to ride them. Although each lift is different, getting on the various lifts is similar. Here are some general guidelines to follow when using any lift:

1 Observe the loading procedure.

2 Whether you are getting on or off a lift, always have your back foot free and resting on the stomp pad.

3 Skate onto the loading area and face the oncoming lift.

4 Board the lift as instructed by the attendant.

5 When unloading avoid traffic congestion by skating out of the unloading area as quickly and safely as possible.

SUR face Lifts

(R O P E   T O W ,   T - B A R ,   P O M A ,   A N D   P L A T T E R)

1

2

3

4

Surface lifts are more challenging for a beginner. There are four main types: Rope tow, T-bar, Poma, and Platter. The Poma and Platter refer to the type of pulley or handle used. Poma, Platter, and rope tows accommodate one rider at a time. T-bars are for two. If you are solo on a T-bar you can place the bar between your legs or behind your bottom. Since your natural stance on the board is to face sideways, placing the T-bar between your legs is an easy position to be in for your ride up the hill. However on the first day, if you have the option, I recommend you use slopes accessible by a chair lift or, better yet, a gondola. Try the surface lift after you have gained confidence in your riding abilities.

Glossary

Surface lifts: There are four main types – Rope tow, T-bar, Poma, and Platter. The Poma and Platter refer to the type of pulley or handle used. Poma, Platter, and rope tows accommodate one rider at a time. T-bars are for two.

getting on surface lifts

Always observe the loading procedure while in the lift line. When you are getting on and off any lift, have your back foot free and resting on the stomp pad. If you are a little nervous, explain to the lift operator that this is your first time. Move onto the loading area and turn to face the oncoming lift. Remember the more you double up on a T-bar the shorter the lifts are for everyone.

Keep in mind that the lift is moving faster than you are, so you will experience a strong initial pull. Be prepared for this and stay balanced and committed. Don't sit down. The lift is there to pull you up the hill, not to support your weight.

COPING WITH **DIFFICULT TERRAIN** ON THE **LIFT TRACK**

Once on the lift, you now have to deal with the fall line, the bumpy terrain, and the snow conditions. When the pitch is a little off the fall line, you may find your board being pulled off track. Don't panic. Use your edges to compensate and steer your board back. Since your back foot is free and resting in between the bindings, steer the board more with your front foot. Before getting on the lift, you can practice this steering technique on the flats. Your edging and pivoting skills will give you more control when adjusting to the fall line. As you ride up the lift, the pitch and terrain will vary slightly. To remain balanced, keep centered over the board by adjusting your stance. Absorb bumpy terrain ("whoop dee doos") with flexed knees and ankles, and for icy tracks be aggressive with your edges.

getting off SURFACE LIFTS

Once you are at the top of the lift, release the T-bar safely. Be aware of those around you and don't sling shot the T-bar around the bull wheel. Once off, skate out of the unloading area.

GLOSSARY

Whoop de doos: Bumpy terrain.

CHAIR Lifts

Getting ON the CHAIR Lift

Remember the basics. Skate into the lift line and observe the loading procedures. Skate onto the loading area and face the oncoming chair. As the chair reaches you, sit down and lower the safety bar. Enjoy the ride. Along with the basics, here are a few insights that will make your ride even more enjoyable. If your stance is goofy, sit on the far left. If you are regular, sit on the far right. This allows you to keep your board sideways comfortably without resting it across someone else's board or skis. To take the hanging weight off your knee, rest your board on the foot bar, or put your back foot under the tail to support the weight. If you find the unloading speed to be too fast for you, ask the lift attendant to slow it down. They commonly do so for beginners.

1

2

3

getting off the chair lift

Getting off the chair lift can be a
little tricky, but not if you take a
few minutes to prepare yourself.
Raise the safety bar. Put your back
foot on the stomp pad. Focus on
being centered over both feet.
Look down the ramp and stand up.
Keep the base of your board fairly
flat. To move slowly or simply
stop, drag your back foot's toe
or heel over the board's edge.

tips for better boarding

- If your back foot is slipping off your board, make sure you have
a good stomp pad. I like to use a rough one with a good grip.
The rough surface also helps to knock the snow off your boot.

- If you fall going up the T-bar or any tow lift, let go and roll
off the track. If the T-bar is between your legs and dragging
you, don't panic. Just release it and roll off the track.

6

to turn is to learn

basic turns

ou're comfortable with your equipment, you're confident in your ability and you're aching to turn that board and ride the mountain. Well, here are some exercises to get you from the top to the bottom and beyond. The Garland and the Wave help you work on your pivoting and pressure skills – initiating and completing a turn; the isolated skidded turn puts your edge skills to the test – speed control; and the Link allows you to put it all together and sets you up for the next challenge – carving. For these exercises, try a wide, green run.

the garland

A collection of incomplete turns, the Garland (see diagram) provides an effective exercise for practicing initiation and completion phases of a turn repeatedly, and helps develop pivoting skills.
As you traverse across the fall line, play with the pressure in your feet. Increase and decrease the edge angle. Apply pressure to your front foot to steer the board slightly down the fall line, then even out the pressure on both feet to steer it back across the fall line. Repeat.

Basically, you start a turn then change pressure to traverse. As you gain confidence, increase your speed and commitment to the fall line. Look where you want to go. Keep your upper body quiet. Use only a subtle amount of pressure. Focus on steering with your feet. Roll over and practice on the other edge side. When you are on the toe side, think front toe – then both toes. On the heel side, think front heel – then both heels. Build on that rhythm.

glossary

Garland: An exercise represented by a collection of incomplete turns. / **Wave:** Similar to the Garland except larger, it allows you to experience a turn without changing edges.

the **wave**

1

7

This is one of my favorite exercises for working up to a turn. Similar to the Garland except larger, it allows you to experience a turn without changing edges. A medium or long radius traverse with a slow controlled pivot and a slight uphill stop is your goal. With some speed, traverse across the hill. To turn, keep the pressure on the front foot. While sweeping the tail up hill with your back foot, equalize the pressure in both feet and come to a slow stop. Repeat. This simulates the experience of initiation and completion, the start and finish of a turn, without changing edges. The key to controlling the pivot is playing with the pressure in your feet.

You will gradually work towards putting more and more of the board into the fall line and eventually do an isolated turn. This will improve your pivoting skills, and help you overcome any trepidation you may have about the fall line's gradient. Practice on both edges.

2

6

3

4

5

THE ISOLATED SKIDDED TURN

YOUR FIRST TURN

In the previous exercises, you learned how to steer with your feet and pivot your board. Now you have the necessary skills needed to complete a turn. The board's sidecut and flex are designed to make turning easy. All you have to do is have patience, commit yourself, and change your edge.

I have broken down the turn into three parts: initiation, execution and completion (see diagram). Once you master the flow of the turn, you will be ready to link your turns.

Initiation

Execution

Completion

INITIATION

Begin a Wave or Garland. Feel comfortable with and in control of your speed. Commit yourself to the turn.

EXECUTION

When the board is completely in the fall line, your board will be flat. Bend your front knee, apply pressure to your front foot and sweep the tail around with your back foot. Look in the direction you are turning. Push down on your front big toe or heel to aid the pivot. As the board passes through the fall line, steer the board onto the opposite edge.

COMPLETION

As you come onto the new edge, equalize the pressure, flex your knees and come to a controlled stop. Congratulations!

After you have completed a turn, repeat the sequence on the other edge. It is important to be able to isolate the turns before attempting to link them up.

For extra confidence and fun, have a friend pull you around on the flats, and practice steering and changing your edges.

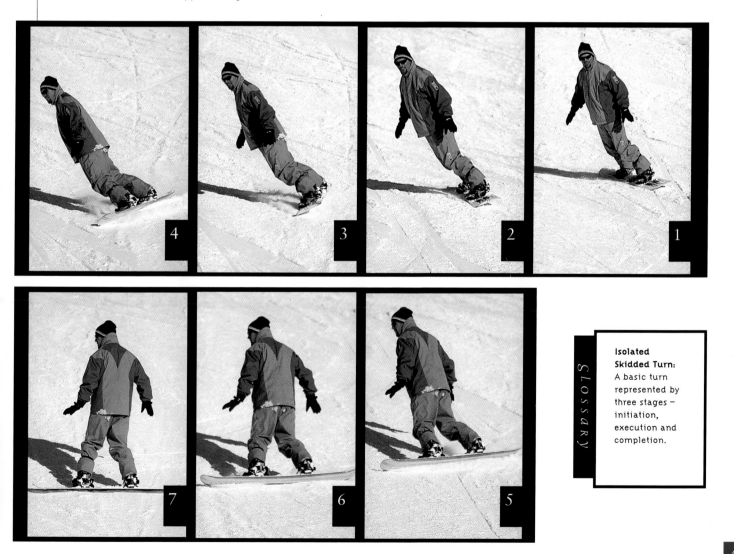

4 3 2 1

7 6 5

Isolated Skidded Turn: A basic turn represented by three stages – initiation, execution and completion.

Glossary

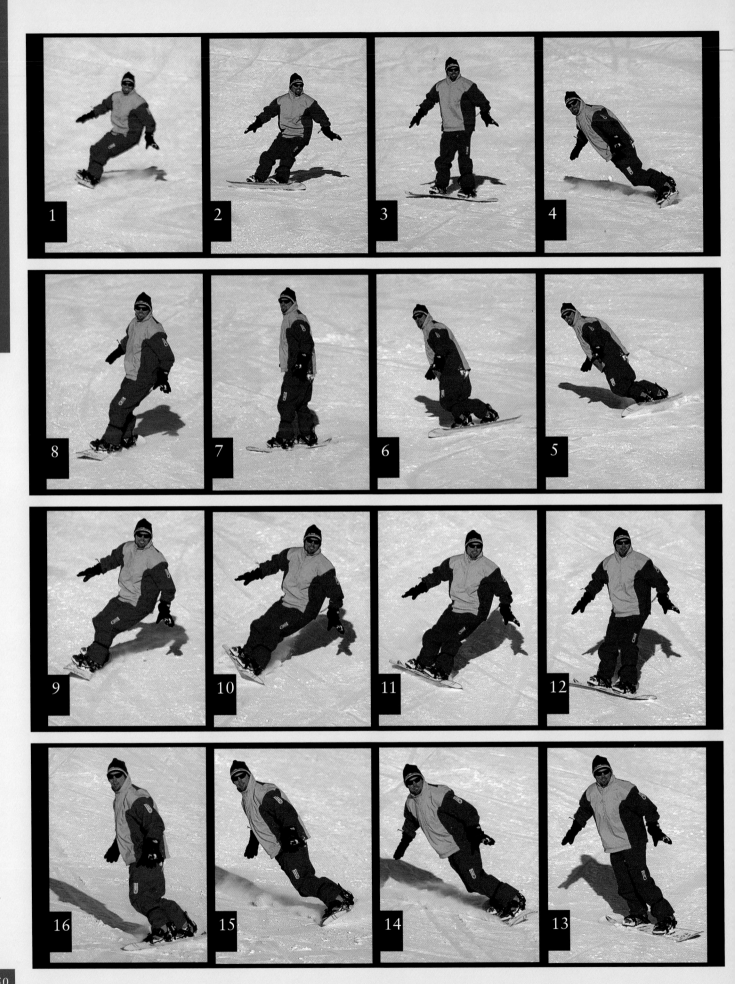

the Link - joining the turns together

Once you can complete isolated turns on both edges with confidence, the next step is to link them. Essentially, you link isolated turns with a traverse in the middle. The traverse allows you time to slow down, get mentally prepared, and set up for the next turn. Following someone else's turns in the snow can sometimes help and guide you. After you start linking turns and cruising around the mountain (with a monster smile on your face), you will start to develop other snowboarding skills, such as speed control and shaping your turns.

Controlling speed

Many riders can't control their speed and end up riding on the edge, out of control the entire time, and this becomes a style they adopt. It is more difficult to be in control and adjust your speed than it is to ride fast. However, if you learn to control your speed, you can advance to steeper runs and new terrain. Increase speed only when your skill level increases.

To understand how to control speed, think about these laws of nature. The more time your board spends in the fall line, the faster you will go. If your board is completely across the fall line, you will stop. A rule of thumb is to always finish your turns and control your speed by adjusting the skid. The challenge is finding the balance between how much or how little to skid the board through the turn. This skill will come with practice as you develop your pivoting and edging skills.

If you apply more pressure to the front foot and increase your edge, the board will skid more across the hill, slowing you down. If the pressure is equal on both feet and the angle flat, the board will move into the fall line and your speed will increase. As the slope's pitch changes you have to adjust the skid to keep your speed consistent.

Consistency is the key to control. Just remember that any time there is a change in pitch and direction, an adjustment is needed.

Glossary

Skid: A slight drag in the snow while turning or pivoting. Finish your turns and control your speed by adjusting the skid. / **Speed:** The more time your board spends in the fall line, the faster you will go.

VARYING the RADIUS of the TURNS

After you consistently link turns and control your speed, the next step is to flex and extend your knees and ankles at the right time, and in the right sequence. This allows you to initiate your turns with ease, and control pressure on the board through the turn. How much you put the board on edge, and how much and how quick you pressure the board activates the sidecut of the board, which affects the radius.

To put the board on edge, use your ankles and knees. I get my students to think of bending their knees into the hill while on the toe edge, and feeling their calves against the high back or boots on the heel side. These sensations will result in tipping the board on edge. Increasing the edge angle will result in more pressure building up on the board. To control this pressure, you will have to flex your knees, ankles and hips. As you flex and extend through these joints, the pressure transcends to the edge. A large edge angle and substantial pressure will cause the board to do a short radius turn; conversely, a small edge angle and gradual pressure will result in a long radius turn. As an exercise, try to do a series of each, experimenting with your edging and pressure skills.

ROUNDING out your turns

2

3

4

5

6

7

Linking your first turns is magic, and when you attain this goal, you are rewarded with a deep sense of accomplishment. If the round turn eludes you, remember that turns are shaped by how you steer the board through the turn. You can quite often analyze your own tracks in the snow. To see your track clearly, ride some fresh corduroy early in the morning. Do a series of small, medium and large turns (see diagram). From the chair lift you can see the shapes easily . Keep in mind, the more pressure on the front foot, the more the board skids; the more equal the pressure, the less the skid. If all the movements are even and proportionate, the turns will be round and the ride smooth.

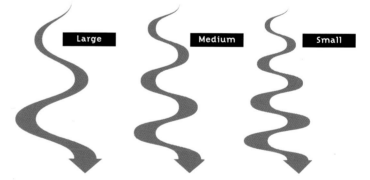

Large   Medium   Small

tips for better boarding

- As you turn, bend your front knee; feel your toe or heel (depending on your edge) in the front boot, then feel the foot go flat. Your pressure is in the front foot, but do not move your weight over the front foot. Remain centered with only a slight amount of pressure in that front foot.
- Keep your speed under control.
- Find the appropriate terrain for your skill level.

- Stance and balance are the cornerstones to expert snowboarding.
- If you are having trouble sliding smoothly, review your pivoting skills.
- Commit to the fall line.
- Flex your knees and keep your upper body tall and straight.
- Extend, pivot and flex.
- Feel confident about what you are doing before you move on.

7

aDVANCED tURNS
WORKINC UP to tHE cARVE
AND BEYOND

working up to the carve is all about improving your edging skill. As a beginner, you skidded or slid through your turns while trying to vary your radius and control your speed. The carve is where all that hard work pays off. Carving, the speed discipline of snowboarding, is turn and edge control. There is no skidding as the board changes quickly from edge-to-edge. To work up to the carve, start with the "slarve": part slide, part carve. A good sliding turn is just as important as a good carve and allows you to adapt to changing terrain. Once you have developed your edging and pressure skills, you will be happily performing the Dynamic Carve, Jet Turning, Eurocarving, and 360s. You may feel as passionate about carving as one of the top ISF (International Snowboarding Federation) snowboarders, Amy Lundstrom: "I let my body do what it is carving to do, turn to turn, edge-to-edge and I fly."

the slarve (part slide, part carve)

If you keep too much weight over the front foot, this causes the board to slide. To reduce the skid in your turn and put more carve in it, begin to equalize the pressure in both feet and use your edges more. Start with a long radius turn. Build up your speed. Work on the timing of your edge-to-edge movement, and play with the amount of pressure in your feet. When you carve perfectly there is no slide (the pressure in your feet is equal) but sometimes you have to let the board slide to adjust to varying snow conditions and terrain, such as moguls, steeps, powder, trees, etc. This is why the Slarve is an important step in learning to carve the hill.

the carve turn

developing edge AND pressure skills

The pure carve turn has no slide or skid. No slide means quick edge-to-edge performance, quick movements in the ankles, knees, and hips and equal pressure in the feet. A pure carve leaves an arc or rut in the snow.

To advance to the carve, follow these exercises. When you can link sliding turns confidently, control speed and change radius, you are ready to carve.

edge angle exercise

Most beginners have difficulty developing the edging skills for this dynamic move. You must put the board on edge quickly or there's no carve. To develop this skill, traverse across the hill, increasing and decreasing the edge angle. Play with your edge angle, or what I refer to as the gas pedal. Let your ankles and knees do the work.

To stay more centered over your feet, keep your knees and ankles bent, and don't lean over. In soft snow, create less of an angle; in hard snow, create more. If you ride in soft boots, use the forward lean in your high back binding for a more responsive stance.

garLand

Remember this exercise when you were learning sliding turns? Use it here for developing your edging skills. Once you can quickly and confidently put the board on edge, try to hold the edge longer, and, to avoid sliding, keep the pressure equal over both feet. Gradually hold the carve longer and allow the board to find the fall line a little more.

wave

This is a natural extension of the previous exercise. Do the same thing, but hold the carve even longer. To benefit from the wave exercise, practice on wide open runs. Keep your upper body upright. Stay centered over the board with your knees and ankles flexed.

isoLated carved tURN

Continue to practice the wave, but this time try to change edges. Traverse with a flat board until you have appropriate speed. Tip the board onto an edge, balance your foot pressure equally on the edge, ride the sidecut, and finish the turn across the fall line or slightly uphill. Practice with an isolated carve on both edges until you feel confident before you link them.

LINKING the carved tURN

Go to a gentle slope and start out with a long radius turn. Use your knees and ankles to unweight the board (think of them as shock absorbers) and pick up speed. Apply equal pressure in both feet; bend at the knees and ankles (compress); and incline slightly into the hill. Snap out of the turn (extend), and begin your next traverse to a carved turn.

HOW to CONTROL speed WHEN DOING carved tURNS

A carved turn is very efficient and the result is more speed. Since there is no slide in your turns, you will gain speed quickly, especially on steep runs. Stay on easy runs while developing your carving skills before venturing onto more challenging runs. There are two ways to control your speed; one, perform long radius turns across the fall line; and two, let the board slide slightly. It is not a sin to slide. Even the expert carver is challenged constantly with speed control.

gLossary

Compress: Bend at the knees and ankles. / **Extend:** A vertical move, stretching through knees, ankles, and hips to unweight the board.

DYNAMIC CARVING

ADDING THE PRESSURE SKILL

4   3   2   1

5   6   7   8

There is much mileage to cover between learning to carve and dynamic carving. Don't get discouraged, you'll get there. Once you start linking, try experimenting with the flexion and extension of your lower body. This will help you get the performance out of each turn.

9   10   11

A snowboard has power potential in its camber, deep sidecut and flex. To use these features to your advantage, you must be able to pressure the board or "bend the board." As you flex through the turns, the board will respond. For example, as you pressure the board through or during the turn, it will rocket you out of a turn as you extend your knees and ankles to unweight it. Practice with long, medium and short radius turns. If you just put the board on its edge and ride the sidecut, the radius carved will be the board's. To control the turn's size and shape, you must increase the edge angle and pressure through the turn. You may want to do isolated turns or the wave to practice. The idea is to gradually add compression and extension in the turns. As you feel the pressure on the board build up, compress your knees and ankles proportionally. As you begin to feel the pressure ease off, extend through the same joints. When these movements are performed at the right time and in sequence, you will have carved your first dynamic turn.

BODY POSITIONING - ANGULATION VS. INCLINATION

With increased speed and a larger edge angle through a dynamic carve, a balanced body position becomes more challenging. When initiating turns, boarders incline or lean into their turns. It only feels natural to do this, and it feels great! Due to the width of the snowboard it is possible to create large edge angles. Inclining into your turns can unfortunately be proportionate to this angle. Leaning too far into your turn can leave you in a vulnerable position and rob you of your balance. When large edge angles are created either the boarder inclines way too much and wipes out, or skillfully adjusts to stay balanced over the edge.

The skillful adjustment is what you want to be able to do. First, understand the difference between angulation and inclination. Body angulation is created from the board edge upward, involves your lower body, and should be proportionate to the edge angle of the board, allowing the upper body to remain upright and centered over the board. When you incline, you lean your body into the hill. The correct body angle needed to assist in the completion of the turn is created in the knees, ankles, and hips, while the upper body remains level with the slope. If you feel yourself inclining too much, adjust your angulation to compensate.

JET TURNING - USING the tail of the BOARD

With these turns, you adjust your weight forward and then rock back to the tail. You apply pressure to the board from tip to tail. A subtle, fluid move that should be left to the expert who has full understanding of stance and balance. The trick is to maximize the effective edge by powering off the tail at the end of the turn, then quickly shifting your weight to just forward of center. To simulate the move, try it static with a flat base. To practice these turns, start with one turn at a time. As you start the turn, adjust your weight slightly forward of center, then move back to center during the middle of the turn, and back from center as you finish the turn. Think about adjusting your stance and balance fore and aft. Add a bit of air at the end of the turn for style.

Glossary

Body angulation: Created from the board edge upward involves your lower body and should be proportionate to the edge angle of the board, allowing the upper body to remain upright and centered over the board. / **Jet Turning:** Using the tail of the board for sudden, powerful ends to turns. You apply pressure to the board from tip to tail. A subtle, fluid move that should be left to the expert who has full understanding of stance and balance. / **Inclination:** Leaning your body into the hill as you carve.

1

2

8

3

7

Layed out carves

eurocarving and the "vitelli turn"

This turn evolved from the European riders and involves increasing your inclination. Your competence in adjusting your angulation, snapping in and out the carve, and controlling your speed, dictates your success with the "Vitelli Turn." You must have sufficient speed to provide stability on the edge angles. Start by doing your regular carved turns, then play with the amount of inclination. With time you will be carving at high speed, scraping the surface of the snow and banking or leaning into the hill like an expert Eurocarver.

4

6

5

0° 36° 72° 108°

the CARVING 360

144° 180° 216° 252°

288° 324° 360°

The key here is to find an area with the right terrain. You will need a steep pitch that mellows out to an easy run. Haul ass down the steep pitch, tip the board on edge and ride the sidecut as long as you can. Stay balanced. As a progression to the carving 360, start with a 180 carve, then go to a 270, and then 360.

Glossary

Eurocarving: This turn evolved from the European riders and involves increasing your inclination. With time you will be carving at high speed, scraping the surface of the snow and banking or leaning into the hill like an expert Eurocarver. / **The Carving 360:** Haul ass down the steep pitch, then tip the board on edge and ride the sidecut as long as you can.

tips for better boarding

- Always go back to the angulation/inclination relationship.
  Also, equal pressure on both feet creates a true carve.

8

RIDING varied terrain

COPING WITH DIFFICULT CONDITIONS

*m*ost people, after they learn how to snowboard, quickly find their favorite hit run, carving run, or preferred area of the mountain. There is absolutely nothing wrong with doing the same runs over and over as long as you're having a good time. However, you might find that you stop progressing once your favorite runs are no longer a challenge. You might even get bored! If you're the kind of person who always wants to keep things interesting then I would alter your approach to the mountain slightly. A couple of things helped me keep my snowboarding fresh and interesting, even after ten years; one, by becoming a versatile rider on varied snow conditions and terrain, and two, knowing how to get the most out of my equipment.

One of the first steps to becoming a versatile snowboarder is to be able to ride varied terrain and snow conditions. If you're one of those people who hate the ice, avoid moguls, or can't ride down a double black, then there are still a few things for you to learn. Read on.

When you ride steeper terrain, you use the same skills as you did in previous turns on gentler slopes. Steep terrain is relative to your ability. As you gain more confidence, it is natural to explore more challenging runs. To perform with ease, your skills need to be strong and your ability to make adjustments in all areas, sharp. Quite often you will experience some of the same difficulties you did when you were doing your very first turns. For example, not committing to the fall line, putting your weight on your back foot, not completing your turns, and losing control of your speed. If you are not progressing, return to an easier run. When I can't find any weakness in someone's riding, I put them on steeper terrain, and then all their bad habits come back. The challenges remain the same: control your speed, commit, always finish the turn, and watch your stance and balance.

To prepare yourself for the steeps, gradually work your way up to more challenging terrain. Tackle the slope where you practiced your first turns. Do a turn. Then traverse until you are confident about the next turn. Gradually work up to a fluid series of turns.

Here are some new and old tips: Stay centered and balanced over your board. Keep your arms and shoulders up for balance. Lazy hands dangling around your sides won't cut it on steep terrain. Keep knees and ankles flexed, creating a lower center of gravity. Open up your knees and legs to a wider stance: this will ensure maximum edge contact and pressure over the entire board for a stable platform. Your upper body should remain tall and upright. Commit and turn the board with confidence. A fall or mistake here can be severe, so balance is key.

Once you have initiated the turn and committed with confidence, don't put your weight on your back foot. To control your speed, always finish the turn and keep the board out of the fall line as much as possible.

Glossary

Dynamic turns: Quick movements and carving in the lower body for sharp, powerful movement.
Steeps: Significantly sloped sections of a mountain.

1

2

3

open sLopes aND couLoirs

These slopes are found in the high alpine and boast the most challenging terrain. This is where you are actually riding the mountain. Providing the snow conditions are good, open slopes or bowls allow you more room to initiate turns. Open slopes are great for large, wide turns. Couloirs, or narrow steep runs, call for shorter radius turns.

When you drop into a couloir, you have a limited amount of room in which to turn, and you may have to perform jump turns. This will require dynamic pressure skills. The only way to jump off the ground, whether on the flats or steeps, is to spring off your knees. A strong flexion and extension through the knees and ankles is required. The steeper pitch can work to your advantage, as there is less distance to travel to unweight your board. But quick adjustment is key.

4

5

6

moGuLs

Very challenging and often too difficult for most snowboarders, riding moguls requires expert balance and the ability to adapt quickly to terrain changes. The best bump riders always look ahead, have complete control of their lower body, are relaxed and have aggressive rhythm.

As always, good stance and balance are crucial. Since you are performing turns in the fall line, it will help if you adjust your stance to face the direction of travel down the hill. This may require a slight twist in the upper body. If you plan to be a mogul expert, I would encourage appropriate forward angle adjustment in your bindings (30°/10°), allowing you to face the direction of travel comfortably .

Once you are facing the direction of travel comfortably pick out your line of travel. To negotiate terrain changes and varying snow conditions you need to know at least two to three bumps ahead where you are going to turn. All too often boarders get off track and end up riding across the run in a criss-cross fashion. Anticipate your movements and visualize the flow. Make it easy on yourself; turn at every bump or at every second bump and focus on a straight line. And if you haven't mastered a quick short radius turn, go home. You will be forced to turn quickly, with dynamic, short radius turns. For a quick pivot, lift the tail of your board on each turn. The sensation you are looking for is a lightness in the tail. Don't lean too far forward. To control speed, you must minimize the amount of time your board is in the fall line. This is done by skidding your turns across the hill more, or on the bump, and using maximum edge angle. Sideslip or traverse off to the side if you get in big trouble. Keeping the board on the snow will help you stay in control. You need to absorb the impact with your lower body.

PICKING appropriate BUMPS

Keep in mind, there are degrees to bumpy terrain. Select an easy run to start, one that will assist you in turning. An ideal pitch is 20 to 30 degrees. The wider spaced bumps are the easiest to ride and control speed. I suggest, at first, you pick well spaced, small rounded bumps on a green slope. If you look at the sides of any bump run you will discover which ones are smaller. As you gain confidence, move onto more challenging bumps. Your technique remains the same regardless, but it becomes harder to control speed in the steeper, tighter and more varied terrain.

Glossary

Couloirs: Narrow steep runs, calling for shorter radius turns. / **Green slope:** A beginner's slope for the easiest run and terrain. / **Jump turns:** Pivoting turns while airborne. The only way to jump off the ground, whether on the flats or steeps, is to spring off your knees. A strong flexion and extension through the knees and ankles is required. / **Moguls:** bumpy terrain, requiring expert balance and very fast response. / **Open slopes:** Wide, clear sections of the mountain, great for large, wide turns.

There are different ways to turn in the bumps: one, in the troughs (ruts between the bumps); two, on the banked sides; three, over the top; and four, hitting the tops.

In the Troughs: Riding through the troughs is the easiest and most popular. You can slide the board easily to slow down, making quicker adjustments to control your speed.

On the Banked Sides: Similar to the ease of the trough, except you turn just above, on the side. This leaves you with less room, so you need to be quick.

On the Top: As you reach the top of the bump, you will feel a little unweighted which aids a quick pivot on the top, and then you slide down the back.

Over the Tops: Caution – only for the expert. As you take your small amount of air off the top of the bump, you change your edge, come down on the new edge and fly, fly, fly. This challenge is for someone who typically runs a straight line in the bump field.

The Combination: Realistically, you will have to adapt your technique to the entire bump field. A constant challenge even for the expert bump rider, this will require a combination of all the techniques discussed above.

trees

Once you have control over your speed and you can adjust your turn shape and radius, riding through the trees will be sheer excitement. Not every ski area has designated tree runs – and in no way am I telling you to go through any set of trees in your local area. In the mountains, snowboarding in the trees or glades is very common and part of the every day experience. When the tree spacing allows for a smooth flowing line and there is fresh powder, the fun begins. Similar to moguls and steeps, trees challenge you to make constant adjustments.

Since trees don't move, are unevenly spaced and you can't go over them or bank them like moguls, you have to make constant adjustments to your speed, your turn shape and rhythm. In the trees, you are forced to turn at certain times, similar to a race course. As with moguls, the line you pick is critical. Always look ahead for the spaces, not the trees, and know where your next turn is.

Always start out in well-spaced trees. Practice mixing up your turns. Be aware of visual objects as you ride on the groomed runs. This will help you be more aware of what is going on around you, such as other skiers, snowboarders, lift towers, snow cats, trees, etc. Be able to increase and decrease speed. Train your eye to read the terrain. You must be able to read the terrain to adapt to it.

1

2

3

deveLopIng tHe eye

perceptIon skILLs

I once had the opportunity to follow the legendary Tom Burt, an extreme technical freerider, for a few days. I wanted to follow his line. After noticing that he usually had the best line, I quickly realized he could scan the terrain and see things that most people miss.

An excellent way to develop this skill is to play "follow the leader." Get in the habit of taking a good look down and around the slope before your run. Learn how to judge speed and distance. This is key to becoming an advanced freerider, especially helpful in avoiding the flats. Read the fall line, where the terrain changes, where you will have to make a transition, a jump, adjust speed, etc. When you can judge speed and distance, it is easier to make the necessary and appropriate adjustments to adapt to changes in the terrain – and you will minimize your time walking the flats!

These are some of the skills
of the expert freerider:
- perception skills
- ability to increase and decrease
  speed when judging distances
- able to adjust turn shape quickly
  to adapt to changes in the terrain

4

5

POWDER

Riding deep powder is epic! Your heart pounds as you choke on powder and lose your sight on every heelside turn. Sounds of a killer session fill the air and fuel the stoke. Trails of cold smoke leave behind many fat tracks. Powder can change your state of mind, make you want to leave your friends behind, quit your job, move to another part of the country, take out a loan and go heli-boarding. Powder junkies say that there are no friends when it comes to powder. To me, powder is the soul of snowboarding and was only ever meant to be the ultimate. I think you get the picture.

The easiest way to get the "feel" of riding powder is straight running in it, with no turning. Usually, after a snow fall, the runs are groomed, but not the sides. The terrain should be pretty mellow and your skills intermediate. Run down these sides. If you fall over, you can easily get back onto the groomed run and start your descent again. Many people start out in a big ol' powder field and end up stuck and frustrated.

When straight running, you will notice how the large surface area of the board, combined with speed, allows it to plane or float on top of the snow. Try bouncing your board. This will give you a better understanding of how the board plays in powder and takes less effort to turn. Since you are not using your edges, your pressure and pivoting skills become less technical and more subtle and fluid.

Keep the weight slightly on your back foot or centered. Don't keep your weight on the front foot or you'll dive over the board's nose into the snow. If you are having trouble keeping your weight back, you might want to mount your bindings slightly back from center. Remember when the powder is two feet deep, there is nothing hard for your edge to bite into, so go with the flow and keep to a run that you're comfortable with before you bust the bank account in search of uncharted powder.

Glossary

Hardpack: Icy snow, packed solid by frequent riders or changes in temperature.
Powder: Fresh, untouched snowfall, preferably very deep and light.

ice / HARDPACK

I used to hate riding in icy conditions, then I realized that I just didn't know how to ride it. For over ten years, I've been snowboarding in mainly ideal conditions. At times it does get icy, but now I love riding the ice. It keeps me on my toes and my technique sharp. Not only do you need to have excellent edging skills, your edges need to be razor sharp to keep you in control. For sheer riding technique, keep the pressure as equal as possible through the turn and your balanced centered. The more pressure you have on your front foot the more the board will skid, something you don't want in icy conditions. If you can't perform pure carved turns, you are going to have trouble with the ice. Slow things down for more control.

The best equipment for icy conditions is hard boots and an alpine board. Hard boots give you extra support, taking on some of the work. Obviously a stiffer board with maximum edge contact is best for stability and control. Sharpen your edges to 88 degrees instead of 90. You can still rip the ice in soft boots on a freestyle board. You just have to work harder. There are now several good freeride boots available that offer the extra support you need, plus give you the freedom to tweak with the best of them. If you're stuck with what you have, you can doctor them up with a power strap or duct tape. Also, I recommend normal high backs, canted inwards for that extra support and a quicker edge response. If you have three straps on your bindings, use them.

If the fast and fun ice runs aren't for you and you find yourself in the middle of one, look for the snow on the sides or patches of snow scattered on the slope. Scan the terrain. Know where you are going to turn and stay in control of your speed.

sLush

I love the slush! The thicker the better. It's consistent and soft, and your riding technique is much the same. Slightly more edge pressure is needed, but it still doesn't hold your edges like hardpack. Slush is easy to control your speed in, landings are soft, and the weather is warm – always a plus. Slush conditions usually occur in the spring when the days are warmer and longer.

Death cookies

Frozen chunks or balls of snow, often hidden beneath new snow, can throw you off balance instantly. Death cookies are part of avalanche debris and can be as big as beach balls. Avoid them. If they take you by surprise, ride them like moguls. Flex your knees. Absorb the irregularities and find a new line of travel.

off piste

Off piste is anywhere off the groomed run. This is anything from off groomed runs in the ski boundary to the backcountry. Off piste also means that you are in an uncontrolled environment: the runs are not groomed, there is no avalanche control, and there is no ski-patrol sweep at the end of the day. In other words, you are taking extra risks. Anything can happen. You could have your best or your worst experience. Snow conditions can change quickly with fluctuating temperatures, creating avalanche conditions. Even if you are in a safe area, you could twist an ankle or get hypothermia, and there is no safety patrol to rescue you. These are the dangers. Be aware.

One reason to go off piste is to have an extremely satisfying powder experience. To ensure you enjoy one, take a buddy or three or more. Know where you are going and the weather forecast for that area. Tell someone at home your destination and your estimated time of return. Dress the part and layer it: underwear, fleece, outer shell, gloves, hat, etc. Pack food, water and extra clothing. Have the right gear and know how to use it. Be self-reliant.

Terrain and length of trip will dictate how much food, water and gear you need, but make sure it's practical and light weight. A heavy pack will not only exhaust you, it'll send you face-first into the powder. Here's a checklist of gear you should always carry with you, whether your trip off piste is merely a search for powder out of bounds at a resort or high into the backcountry:

1 **An avalanche transceiver (Pieps).** Pieps send out a signal that could save your life if you get buried. Keep it close to your body and know how to use it. Everyone in the group should have one.

2 **Ski pole(s).** Ski poles are helpful when climbing and can be used as an avalanche probe. Get the collapsible kind so you can store them in your pack.

3 **A shovel.** Once you've located your buried buddy, you'll need something to dig him or her out, and a snowboard won't cut it. To make sure you don't destroy any air pockets, dig at an angle. You've got two minutes.

4 **Snowshoes.** Small and light and easy to carry on your pack, snowshoes help you hike in deep snow and you can wear soft boots with them.

5 **Goggles, sunglasses and sunscreen** – stuff for the blinding, burning sun.

6 **Extra clothing** such as hat, mitts, socks, fleece.

7 **Water.** Stay hydrated.

8 **Food.** For short trips, pack quick energy food, such as fruit, trail mix, power bars, power drink, etc.

9 **First Aid kit.**

10 **Your longest board.** You'll be riding deep powder so set your bindings back a bit.

Other items you might need, depending on your trip, include: an ice axe, crampons, rope, jackknife, extra screws and parts for your snowboard bindings, string, tent, sleeping bag, cooking gear, and extra clothing. If it's an expedition you're on, sneak the heavy gear into your buddies' packs and smile on.

One last word of caution: Each year, over 100 people are caught in avalanches, and, on average, 24 never return alive.

Glossary

Off piste: Anywhere off the groomed run.
Pieps: An avalanche tranceiver.

tips for better boarding

- Understand speed control. You should be comfortable with your speed at the end of each turn, and your speed should be consistent and not building after every turn.

- In challenging snow conditions such as ice, flex through the knees and ankles to control the pressure on the board and edges.

- Maintain a quiet upper body. Don't throw your arms and upper body around. Keep your arms up and level with the slope in a balanced position.

COULOIRS AND STEEPS

- Always have an entrance and exit plan for a couloir and a steep open slope. Know the safe route in and out in case of avalanche possibilities or other potential dangers. Leave room for error. Remember you don't have to risk your life to have fun.

MOGULS

- The trouble with moguls is you have to make quick turns. Most people can't turn fast enough. A dynamic, short radius turn is a must. Keep your speed under control. Absorption in the lower body is critical.

TREES

- For trees, match your ability with the density of the trees. Start with open spaced trees.

POWDER

- Most people, especially alpine riders, try to edge too much, as if they were riding on groomed or hard packed snow. Don't lean too far forward or else your board will dive into the snow.

ICE AND HARD PACK

- Sharpen your edges to 88 degrees. Adjust your highbacks to a forward lean. Develop your edging skills.

SLUSH

- Less edging.

DEATH COOKIES

- Avoid them.

OFF PISTE

- Educate yourself about the backcountry. Too many 'boarders are lured into the backcountry in search of powder without the proper knowledge or equipment to survive. Take courses. Get the proper equipment, and plan ahead in order to stay safe.

9

BASIC freestyle

to air is human

f reestyle is the most popular style of snowboarding. Many young riders try to fly before they can even turn properly, and who can blame them? Influenced by skateboarding, these tricks and maneuvers satisfy that primal urge to defy gravity. Always evolving, the discipline of freestyle is taken to new levels every winter by the best snowboarders in the world. By the time you read this, new cool tricks will have replaced the old ones. However, the basic techniques for catching air never change, and classics are always a challenge to perform. Once you have a solid grounding in the basics, be free to create your own style – freestyle it! I suggest you have good intermediate freeriding skills before you attempt airs and tricks. This will allow you to progress faster and more naturally. Develop your all-round snowboard skills. Have fun and do what comes natural. When learning anything new, always keep safety in mind.

some flatland basics

SPINS ON THE SNOW

180 DEGREES AND 360 DEGREES

A 180 degree spin on the snow is merely sliding the board around 180 degrees to a controlled stop. Think about doing a normal, slow sliding turn, but continue the slide until you are riding backwards, then come to a slow stop. Keep a centered stance, look in the direction you want to rotate, steer with the feet and change edges. Begin by pressuring the front foot to turn. At the end of the turn, pressure the back foot and look where you want to go. The board will turn 180 degrees.

Spinning 360 degrees is the same as doing two 180s. This time you change your edges twice, shifting the pressure back and forth. Once you have completed the first 180, transfer the pressure back to the front foot. The board will continue to pivot around, completing a 360 degree spin. When going backwards, the back foot now becomes the leading foot to pivot off.

Glossary

180: A 180 degree spin on the snow is merely sliding the board around 180 degrees to a controlled stop.
360: The same as doing two 180 degree spins.

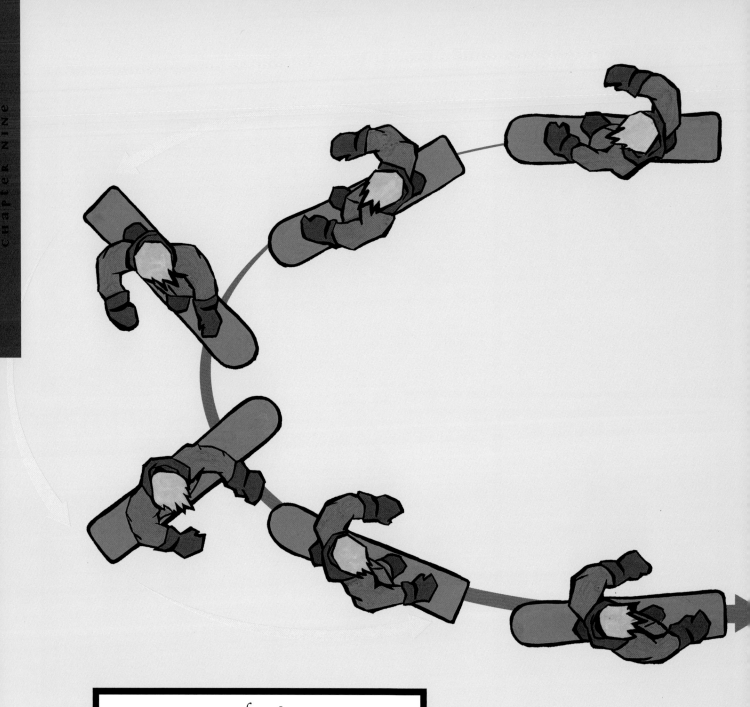

RIDING fakie

Riding fakie (backwards) is one of the most important and fundamental skills of freestyle snowboarding. Anything you can do forwards you can do backwards. Riding fakie opens up twice as many possibilities. The best way to understand riding fakie is to imagine doing everything opposite to riding forwards. You're still thinking about the same things, except you are now traveling in the opposite direction. Stay centered, pivot around your leading foot, which is now the back foot. Look where you are going. The same problems you had when you were learning will surface when learning how to ride fakie. Use all the same exercises you did when learning how to turn (refer back to Chapter 4 if you need to refresh your memory). Go slowly and stay in control.

n o s e AND t a i L ROLLs

On the flats, practice balancing on the tail and nose of your board. Experiment and get a feel for how the board flexes as you attempt to balance on the tail and on the nose.

When performing a nose roll, you roll or spin off the nose. Ride forward with a flat base, and then move your hips forward quickly and rotate your upper body in the desired direction. Think about pivoting off the front foot. The only part of the board that remains on the ground is the nose. Practice on a small bank, or berm. To add more cha llenge, try to spring off the nose and catch a little air. As you become more comfortable with nose rolls, catching air will come naturally.

For tail rolls, ride fakie. Very similar to the nose roll, except this time, the only part of the board that stays on the ground is the tail. Load up the tail with pressure, keep your base flat, release the pressure and pivot around the back foot. Timing is key here. Use your upper body to help the rotation, equalize the pressure, and re-center over your feet. Think of spinning around the tail. Look in the desired direction. Go very slow at first to avoid catching an edge. Nose and tail rolls are excellent exercises for 180 airs and half cabs.

w h e e L i e s

Wheelies are not that popular. But hey, if you want to do wheelies, go ahead. On the flats, get used to centering your weight over your back foot. Then, when you're out there riding, sit back and wheelie your board like a motorcycle.

BASIC JUMPS

When you are getting air for the first time, start with "credit card air" or very small air. You want a very gentle jump or simply a small roller. This way, the transition is minimal, and it won't throw you off balance. Landings should be at least as steep as the jump and never flat. Flat landings are too hard on the knees.

PREPARATION - Approach the jump or hit with your speed under control. Get into a slightly flexed position, centered over your board. Keep the base of the board flat. Don't bend at the waist.

execution (take off) - Jump. Use your arms for balance. Extend your legs, and then bring your knees towards your chest. Don't bring your chest to meet your knees. Keep compressed in the air. Stay centered. Spot your landing.

COMPLETION (LANDING) - Extend your legs to meet the snow. As you land, keep the same centered position and bend your knees slightly, keeping the base flat. Your lower body will act as your shock absorber. Be relaxed. You will have to adjust your stance to whatever meets your board on impact.

When performing your first jumps, the idea is to feel what it's like to get a little air. You are still traveling at relatively slow speeds and not yet springing off the jump. As you improve, increase your approach speed. To gain height, put some spring into your jump by extending more with your legs. To prolong the jump, bring your knees closer to your chest.

| 5 | 4 | 3 | 2 | 1 |

oLLies

The ollie is one of the essential freestyle basics you must master if you want to be an expert freestyler. Once you have perfected your ollie, it will allow you to re-center and adapt to the transitions faster in the air. It will also allow you to get even more air whether it's a small roller or in the pipe. Practice flatland ollies first. Move your weight over your tail. At this point, your nose and front foot should be slightly off the ground. Then spring up and forward while at the same time bringing your front then back leg up. Your tail should be the last thing off the ground. You are now airborne. Always land centered. Look for things to ollie over or from, such as rollers, small jumps or small children. If you're having trouble, throw yourself forward more, or try jumping on the flats while standing still.

NOLLies

A nollie is a close cousin of the ollie. The only difference is, this time, you spring off the nose. The nollie is a little trickier, and not as useful in my mind, but nevertheless another trick to master. The tricky part is to not throw your weight too far forward. This will cause you to lose your balance.

BONING aND Pokes

This refers to anytime you straighten one leg. If your bindings and high backs restrict your legs from moving laterally, it should be possible to rotate your high backs so they are flush with the edge. This may vary from company to company.

shifties

A shifty is a basic air, where the upper and lower body move in opposite directions. For style, bone out either your back or your front leg.

Glossary

Bone or Poke: Refers to any time you straighten out your leg during an air. / **Credit card air:** Very small air. / **Nollie:** Like an ollie, this time beginning with your board's tail and ending with the board's nose. / **Ollies:** A basic air in which you use your legs to pull the nose of your board up, followed by the waist and tail in one smooth motion. / **Shifty:** Moving the upper and lower body in opposite directions during an air. / **Stiffy:** Any air where you straighten both legs in front of you. **Transition:** The curve between the flat and the lip of a pipe wall or jump.

stiffies

The name stiffy says it all. Any air where you straighten both legs in front of you. Raise them up as far as you can.

Glossary

Stiffy: Any air where you straighten both legs in front of you.
Grabbed Airs: Derived from the world of skateboarding, where the rider grabs the board to hold it in place and stabilize it.
Indy Grab: Grabbing the board toe edge between your feet with your back hand. / **Mute Air:** Grabbing the board's toe edge with your front hand and doing a shifty sideways.

BASIC GRABBED AIRS

Grabbed airs come from the world of skateboarding, where the rider grabs the board to hold it in place and stabilize it. When you're snowboarding, you are also stabilizing your board, but you're adding a new challenge to your airs. Before you attempt one, make sure you can do basic lofty airs without grabs. Start with the easy grabs, which allow you to stay centered over your board and don't involve much movement or contortion. At the beginning, grab your board where and when it feels natural. And don't reach for your board, bring it to you.

mute AIR

Grab your toe edge with your front hand. This is one of the easier moves but it is essential to stay centered.

80

4

3

2

5

the **INDY** GRAB

One of the easiest grabbed airs to do. Bring the board to your chest and grab the board toe edge between your feet with your back hand. For the extra challenge, bone the front leg.

6

1

7

method air

A method air is the most classic air ever and always will be. As you kick up your board behind you, grab heel side with your front hand. The sequence shows a more advanced frontside 360 turn ending with a method air.

SPINS IN THE AIR

When learning to spin in the air, it is important to understand the basic mechanics of a rotation.

PREPARATION - Have your speed under control. Stay centered and balanced. Focus on the transition, approach the jump low and compact.

INITIATION - Wind up your upper body in the opposite way you are going to spin. This wind up is proportionate to the degree of rotation. For example, a 180 will require less wind up than a 540. With practice, you will become a good judge of how much is necessary.

EXECUTION - If you are spinning off the edge, extend through your knees and ankles. If you are riding your base flat, then ollie and begin your rotation. Hold the rotation by unwinding, then anticipate and spot your landing.

COMPLETION - As you spot the landing, open up from your tucked position to slow down your rotation. From here, it's just like landing a regular straight air.

Glossary

Method Air: Kicking up your board behind you while grabbing heel side with your front hand. **Spins:** A rotation while in the air.

To stop a spin, stop moving your upper body and focus on a fixed point. This is referred to as "spotting your landing." You should always be aware of your landing area. By spotting your landing, however, you will naturally open up and stop rotating. Since your lower body follows your upper body, spotting your landing will minimize over rotating. To slow down the spin, open up your body. Think about a figure skater who opens up the spin to slow down and brings the arms and body into a tighter position to speed up and continue the rotation. For more spin, stay tucked longer.

air to fakie

Before trying this trick, learn to ride fakie. Independent "leg action" starts to become a little more important. Carve the board toe edge across the fall line. Transfer pressure to your front foot, then release pressure by extending through your knees and ankles. Re-center in the air and spot your landing. Land centered with the base flat. For added flair, try pulling a 360 in mid-air, rotating your body in the desired direction. Make sure you can carve your board, railing the sucker with no skid. Why? Because when you are learning to spin it is easier to spin off the edge.

Half cabs

Similar to the Air to Fakie trick, except it's the opposite. Carve the board fakie across the fall line on your toe edge. It's easier to spin off the toe edge. Transfer pressure to your leading foot (now your back foot), extend through your knees and ankles, rotate upper body in the desired direction, center yourself in the air, spot your landing, and land centered. As you gain confidence, add more speed and air, and work into the fall line more.

360s

Doing a 360 is a natural progression from a 180. Again, it is easier to practice across the fall line. You will need more speed to get more air than you used when learning a 180. Carve toe side, lead with head and shoulders, hold rotation. As you almost complete the rotation, spot the landing, center yourself and land flat base. Commitment is important. When you're ready, try taking off and landing fakie, as shown.

caBaLLeRiaLs (switch 360)

This is a 360 degree rotation but you start and finish fakie. This trick was named after the inventor, legendary professional skateboarder Steve Caballero. You should be able to do regular 360s and half cabs confidently before trying this trick.

Late spins

A late spin is when your upper body rotates, but your lower body does not complete the rotation until the last minute. The lower body is held in a static position just prior to landing. The spin really happens at the same time but due to a change in body position – an upper and lower body separation – it looks like things have been slowed down.

540 s

Again, when you do a longer rotation everything is the same except you hold the rotation longer. You over rotate a 360, spot the landing and land fakie. When doing a 540 degree rotation, you will be landing backwards, so it is important that you can ride fakie confidently.

720 s

The 720 requires another level of air awareness (attention and confidence while airborne) and skill. You will have to overcome instinct. Once you see your landing it is natural to stop the rotation. This is what you must overcome. You will see your landing twice; the first time you must ignore it and spot it the second time. At this level, you should know what you're doing, and you won't be following this book any more – you'll be freestyling with confidence!

tHe snowboard park

A snowboard park creates the ultimate freestyle environment. This designated snowboard-only area is fully loaded with jumps, berms, rollers, rails and other obstacles, some natural, but most are man-made jumps. Rails, metal drums and cars are becoming extinct. A good park is like taking all the best hits on the mountain and putting them in one controlled area with loud music. The obstacles in a good park are designed to be interchangeable, to keep it challenging and allow for new freestyle ideas. The better parks label each obstacle's degree of difficulty. For example, an easy obstacle is labeled with a green circle, similar to a green run on a slope, and something challenging is labeled with a black diamond. To make things more comfortable, some resorts have added garbage cans, tools, water and benches to the park.

That said, every park will be different so familiarize yourself with the terrain and the degree of difficulty of the jumps and transitions. Scan the park and wait your turn before you drop in. Look ahead and be aware of your line. Think about maximizing your terrain as you roam through the park. It's a great place to discover freestyle and learn new tricks, but have some basic freestyle down before dropping in.

Glossary

The Park: This designated snowboard-only area is fully loaded with jumps, berms, rollers, rails and other obstacles, some natural, but most are man-made jumps.

tips for better boarding

SPINS ON THE SNOW
- Try not to over rotate. Improve your pivoting skills by practice the Falling Leaf, Garland and the Wave.

RIDING FAKIE
- When riding fakie, you will find that some of the problems you had when first learning to turn will re-surface. Take it slow and practice.

SPINS IN THE AIR
- Spot your landing and commit to the full rotation.

BASIC JUMPS
- Your landing must be as steep as your jump. Avoid flat landings.
- Don't stand while you're in the air; remain compressed and keep your arms quiet.
- Absorb your landing by bending your knees and ankles as much as possible.

GRABS
- Be confident with your basic jumps before you attempt to grab your board. You need to develop your "air awareness."

10

HaLfpipe RIDING

I f you have good air awareness and freeriding skills, it's time to drop in, ride the pipe and launch big air tricks. Dug into the mountain, roughly 3-6 meters deep, 10 to 18 meters wide and about 50 to 110 meters long, the halfpipe includes the flat (the pipe's floor), the transitions (curved section between the floor and the walls), and the walls or the vertical (vert). The top of the wall is called the lip. Outside the pipe is the deck or platform where all your buddies hang to watch you fly or crash. So if you can't carve true arcs in the snow and stay balanced riding up the pipe's transition then go back and work on your basic freestyle skills, because crashing in front of an audience sucks.

adapting to the pipe

Remember, the pipe is in constant use and you can be caught off guard by other riders, rutted walls, worn down transitions, and ice. With that in mind, start your traverse with your eyes wide open. Concentrate on the line you want to take. Look for unused sections that still have vertical on the transition. Spot your turn and ride straight at the wall. While traversing across the pipe's floor, keep your base relatively flat to allow for an easier extension and flexion up and down the transitions. Imagine the vert continuing past the lip of the pipe. This will help you ride straight up and down with ease. Stay in control and increase your height gradually. Focus on riding wall to wall. Get in the habit of spotting where you will turn.

glossary

Backside: Backside is when your back faces the wall. / **Deck:** The platform where people can watch riders perform their tricks along the pipe. / **Flat:** The floor of the pipe. / **Frontside:** Frontside is when you face the wall during the turn or air maneuver. / **Lip:** The top of the pipe wall. / **Transition:** Curved section between the floor and the walls. / **Vertical (vert):** Section of wall top perpendicular to the floor

the frontside and backside wall

The pipe's two walls are called the frontside and the backside, and relate to your position on the board. Frontside is when you face the wall during the turn or air maneuver. If you are regular footed and doing a frontside air, you will approach the right wall. If you are goofy, it will be the left wall.

Backside is when your back faces the wall. If you are regular footed, you will approach the left wall and right if you are goofy.

sLiding tuRNs

To familiarize yourself with riding the transitions, practice sliding turns on the pipe walls. Start by approaching at an angle and gradually work towards riding straight up the transition. Keep the base flat, but use your uphill edge as you ride up the transition.

Do not extend to initiate your turns. As you ride up the wall, you will naturally be unweighted. Pivot the board when you feel lightest and are almost airborne, and ride down the transition.

pumpinG

As you gain confidence with your sliding turns, practice pumping, using your lower and upper body to generate speed. Think of yourself on a swing, leaning back and pushing your legs through the air to gain momentum. This is similar to what you are doing on your board. If you can pump and gain speed, you will be able to increase your air and maximize the trick.

As you ride up the transition, the idea is to be as light on your board as possible, and, at the same time, throw your momentum up the wall. Accomplish this by first being in a compressed position. Then, in a dynamic fashion, extend your knees and ankles as you ride up the transition, throwing your arms and upper body up the wall towards the sky. This will take your weight off the board. As you reach the top of the transition, you should be in a compressed position.

As you ride down, think about directing your energy down the transition. Stay flexed and extend just before the transition ends and across the flat bottom. This will send you across the pipe floor. To prepare for the next wall, get in a flexed position, extend up the next wall and repeat the process. Timing and coordination is key. Take it easy and take each step one at a time.

a I R S

With good air awareness and your pumping and freeriding skills down, riding the pipe and taking air is all about adapting to the pipe. The pipe and its walls will determine when and where you turn, take air and land. So, first, determine your line of travel. Spot your take off and landing. Traverse across the pipe floor on your uphill edge and flatten your board as you ride up the transition. Pump your speed from wall to wall. Imagine the wall continues past the lip. Perform an ollie. Lift your front foot slightly and leave the wall with your back foot. Remain compressed. Spot your landing and put your landing gear down at the top of the vertical, your board pointing down the transition. Pump down the transition and hit the opposite wall.

a I R to f a k I e

This is when you ride up the transition, get air and land fakie. You do not have to rotate or grab in the air, just land centered fakie. A good way to practice getting ready for this trick is to ride fakie, get air, and land fakie when freeriding.

shifties

A shifty is when your upper and lower body move in different directions. These are great airs to do when learning to ride pipe because they don't involve grabs. A shifty can be very stylish, especially if you do a nice lofty one while boning out. Try a backside shifty and bone out the front. Approach as you would a normal air, but, as you take off and gain air, hold your lower body and board in a static position and, using your upper body, look in the desired direction back in the pipe. It's almost like a late spin – just before you land, realign your lower body with your upper body.

stiffies

Stiffies mean straight legs. As the name implies, when you air out of the pipe backside or frontside, you straighten both legs. Don't forget to bend your knees when landing.

pokes and boning

This refers to any time you straighten (bone out) one leg. Boning out the front or back leg can be done with or without a grab, but usually with. To bone or poke is to add another challenge to the air. When attempting to bone while grabbing, try a grabbed air that you are comfortable with. To straighten one leg fully, you must bend the other. While in the air, keep your center of mass over the bent knee as you bone or poke out the free foot.

GRABS

Grabbing your board is a great way to stabilize it while in the air and there are endless variations. Grab the tail, the nose, the heel edge, the toe edge with your front hand or your back hand. Whatever you decide to do, the basic principle is the same: bring your knees up and your board to you, then grab. Never grab just for the sake of grabbing. And try not to be influenced by the current popular tricks. If a grab feels good to you, then it's right and it will help you remain low, compressed, and add challenge. When you are comfortable with grabs, add some spice to the grab by boning (straightening) your front leg, back leg, or both.

There are so many different tricks and names it's impossible and ridiculous to list them all. I have outlined several of the classic and currently popular tricks and maneuvers. A slight variation in the hand position can change the name of a trick. Experiment with various hand positions on your own and may all your airs and grabs feel great and bring you hours of fun.

INDIES

This is when you grab toeside between the feet with your back hand. An Indy Air is great to start out with as it keeps you low and compressed in the air. This grab is a classic and easy to do.

methods

A method is a backside air. Approach the backside wall. Pretend the vert continues past the lip. Bend your knees and kick the board up towards your back, then grab heel edge with your front hand. For style, arch your back or add some of your own spice. Practice this trick without a grab at first, then work into it.

frontside INDY air

Approach the frontside wall and, as you air, bring your knees toward your chest, keeping very compressed, and then grab toeside with rear hand.

stale fish grab

As you air out of the pipe, grab heel edge with your back hand between your feet – not through your legs. Extend your back hand around the back leg. To make this easier, bone out your back leg as much as possible. This trick can be done front or backside.

frontside tail grab

To make it easier to grab your tail, bone out your front leg while you center yourself over the back foot. In this position it should be easy to reach down with your back hand and grab the tail.

mute airs

A mute air can be done frontside or backside but usually the latter, grabbing with the front hand on the toe edge.

Lien air

Done on the frontside wall. Grab heel edge with your front hand slightly in front of the front foot and bone out the back. Since you are now centered over your front foot, it will seem as though you are leaning over the nose.

4

3

5

2

6

INDY poke to fakie

A good introduction to this trick is air to fakie. The trick here is to not allow yourself to rotate. Grab with your rear hand on your toe edge between your feet, then bone out your front leg by sucking your back knee up to your chest while pushing out on your front foot to bone it. For style, try to make your board look flat relative to the ground before you revert back into the pipe fakie.

1

8

7

rotations

There is really no such thing as a half spin in a pipe. A half spin is basically a straight air because you have to do a basic 180 rotation to come back down and re-enter the pipe. A true definition of a rotation in a pipe is a 360 or more. When you do a spin or rotation, there is a good chance you will be landing fakie. To spin slower or faster you can open or close your body similar to a figure skater. Obviously, your head and upper body lead or initiate the spin. Also, it is usually much easier to spin off toeside.

When learning how to spin, it's important to spin on your correct axis. Your torso (belly button area) is the center of every trick. Your torso will remain in the same place regardless of rotation. If you can spin on a fixed axis, this will keep your body leaning into the halfpipe. This changes proportionally with the transition. It is also important to land over the axis. The Rodeo Flip is combination of inverted and spin rotations. If you can understand how this works and put it into practice, your rotations and landing will be much more successful.

glossary

Axis: The central line around which your body spins during a rotation. /
Rotations: Any spin in the air. A true definition of a rotation in a pipe is a 360 or more. / **Torso:** Your upper body around your belly button.

aLLey oop

An Alley Oop is a basic spin trick. The rotation is just slightly more than 180 degrees. Alley Oops are a great way to learn 360s. A frontside Alley Oop is usually a little easier to learn. To make this rotation shorter, ride straight up the transition. As you ride up the transition, sink your edge and spin off toe side. Always spin in the opposite direction to the wall. For example, if you are approaching the frontside wall, spin backside, as shown in this sequence, and vice versa. For style, add an easy grab. Before attempting this maneuver in the pipe, practice on banks when freeriding.

INDY ALLEY OOP

An Alley Oop means the rotation is opposite to the approach or wall. For example, if you approach the frontside wall, you will spin backside. If you approach the backside wall, you will spin frontside. As you spin frontside or backside, grab indy.

FRONTSIDE 360 INDY GRAB

Of all the 360 grabs, this one is probably the easiest one to do. This trick will be almost the same as the frontside 360 Indy, but this time you grab toe edge between your feet with your back hand.

FRONTSIDE 360 METHOD

Ride up the frontside wall. Initiate rotation with your upper body, bend your knees and pull your board behind you. Grab heel edge with your front hand. Hold the grab until you spot the landing, open up and land it.

CABALLIERIALS

As we know from basic freestyle, a Caballerial is a 360 spin in the pipe, starting and landing fakie. This trick is basically a 360 rotation but you start and finish fakie. Practice on the flats prior to the pipe. Approach the transition riding fakie (backside wall toe side may be easiest); as you reach the vert, you are already beginning your rotation. Look where you want to go, bring your knees into chest to stay compressed, hold rotation, spot your landing and ride down the transition fakie. To make this trick a little easier, approach the transition at an angle, making the rotation less than 360 degrees.

FAKIE TO FAKIE 360 INDY

This can be done front or backside. Ride up the transition fakie, and initiate the spin with your upper body. Grab with your new back hand. This means the hand that is normally in front will be executing the grab on your toe edge, between your feet. Hold until rotation is complete, spot your landing and open up to land.

3

2

1

4

5

fRONtSIDe 540

In this trick you will leave riding straight but land fakie. Rotate 540 by first turning 180 to face the direction of travel, then continuing with another 360 rotation. The trick to pulling the last 180 is to remain tucked in the air (compressed) for slightly longer before opening up to slow your rotation. Then, when spotting the landing on the transition, simply let your rear foot drop naturally in front of you to land fakie.

7

6

backside **aLLey** oop

Ride up the frontside wall and spin backside. If you don't grab, it will simply be a backside Alley Oop.

HaNDpLaNts aND iNVeRts

Just like when you learned your first 360 you had to over come a psychological barrier, now your brain will have to get used to your body going upside down. The transition in the pipe helps you get inverted similar to a freestyle ski jump. As with rotations, your head will lead the way. To slow down or speed up, you can open and close your body. A better way to visualize this is being small and tucked or tall and fully extended.

To work up an invert, practice doing hand stands or walking on your hands, with or without your snowboard.

Most handplant tricks have been transplanted from the skateboard world. A handplant is when the rider gets inverted (upside down) above the lip and supports his or her body weight with one hand. Handplants are generally easier on the backside wall.

HaNDpLaNt

Approach the wall with slightly less speed than you would for an air. As with any trick, you will have to gauge your own speed. With a handplant, too much speed will send you out of the pipe and not enough will leave you short of your objective. As you become more familiar with the maneuver, size of pipe, etc., it becomes natural. Throw your head back and your lower body up the transition (similar to a backflip motion). As you invert, your rear hand should be planted firmly on the lip. If you are doing a frontside invert your front hand will be the one supporting you. At this point, remember what it feels like when you were walking on your hands. Although upside down, keep your center of mass centered over your hand. For style, stall and grab your board with your free hand. To re-enter, look back into the pipe and your body will follow. Keep your knees bent until they touch down on the transition. If you are having difficulty with this trick, use two hands and, as you gain confidence, use one.

gLossaRy

Handplant: When the rider gets inverted above the lip and supports his or her body weight with one hand. / **Inverted:** Upside down.

ʙᴀᴄᴋ fʟɪᴘ

Known as "the crippler" in the pipe. A backflip
can of course be done off a kicker freeriding.
Take off on toe edge and commit to the invert
by throwing your head back and bringing your
knees into your chest. The more compressed
you are, the faster you will rotate. Hold
rotation so your body will follow your head.
Resist the temptation to move your head until
the rotation is complete. As you are finishing
your rotation and the world looks familiar
again, untuck and land. If you are in the
pipe, you will most likely land fakie.

3	2	1

RODEO fLIP

This trick combines a 540°
rotation with a backflip.
You will be completely upside
down, spinning 540 degrees
and landing fakie. Needless
to say, if you can do this trick
you won't be reading this book.
It is important to have both
the 540 and the backflip down
before attempting a Rodeo Flip.

5	4

First, throw a frontside 540. Put lots of pepper in the spin. Once you've rotated the first 180, throw your head over your leading shoulder and look towards the top of the pipe, while dropping your back shoulder towards the bottom of the pipe floor. Continue to look around – by 360 degrees it should look like you're going to land on your head. However, if you have done this right, just keep looking and begin to spot your landing, and the board will find itself under your feet, then land and ride away fakie.

TIPS FOR BETTER BOARDING

- Heel edge chattering (backside wall): This is due to low backs, not enough forward lean or not being able to flex properly in the knees and ankles.
- Carving too much on the floor of the pipe: Keep the board's base flat to allow for an easier compression up the transition.
- Ride straight up the pipe wall for maximum air.

- To compensate for a lack of vert, you must be able to ollie effectively.
- Keep your weight centered going up the transition.
- Stay compressed in the air.
- Independent leg action is essential for extending and compressing up and down the transition.

RaCINg

Racing is an extension of riding freely down the mountain. Entry level racers develop their racing skills freeriding on the open slopes. As the rider's skill level progresses, gate training can be gradually introduced and used as a test of the rider's reaction time, sense of rhythm and anxiety level. Competitions are the next step, and serve as an objective measurement of the quality and level of a rider's training.

For many, racing is a recreational activity which may include joining a club and/or competing in local programs. For others, it represents a challenge, to bring their snowboarding skills to an elite level.

This Chapter was written by Bob Allison, currently the program director of the first official snowboard club in Canada, the Blackcomb Snowboard Club in British Columbia, an organization he established and coached in 1992. A former member of the Canadian National Ski Team (1977-79), Bob also established and coached Canada's first National Snowboard Team (1994-95) and helped develop the Racing Module for CASI.

the DISCIPLINES

The sport has evolved into several disciplines: Super Giant Slalom (SG), Giant Slalom (GS), Dual Giant Slalom, Slalom, and Dual Slalom. With the introduction of GS as a medal event in the 1998 Winter Olympics, it is the most frequently run racing discipline, although the exciting Dual events and high speed SG are finding space on more and more schedules.

sLaLom

Slalom is an event requiring the execution of many quick and precise turns. It is run on two different courses marked by triangular panelled gates. The gates are set in varying combinations which test the rider's skill and strategy. A racer's final result is determined by adding the times for both runs.

DuaL sLaLom/giant sLaLom

Dual Slalom/Giant Slalom races may be run on courses resembling Slalom or Giant Slalom and are characterized by two racers riding simultaneously on parallel courses. The races are generally a knockout, with the riders who make it into the finals having raced as many as 16 runs.

giant sLaLom

Giant Slalom is also run on two different courses marked with triangular panelled gates. The courses are run over a faster, longer and more open line down the mountain than slalom. Results are determined by adding the competitor's times for both runs. Giant Slalom tests a rider's ability to maximize use of the terrain.

super giant sLaLom

Super Giant Slalom is relatively new to snowboarding. It is a one-run event demanding courage and judgement as well as technical skills, and is characterized by large turns and changes in terrain. Speeds at the elite level can exceed 55 miles per hour, therefore extensive safety features are incorporated to protect the competitors.

BASIC RIDING SKILLS

Basic riding skills include stance, turn initiation, edging, and timing. The skills are a general guideline and will be adapted for the different types of turns (SL, GS and SG), as well as terrain and snow conditions. These skills will prepare any rider for racing, providing a good understanding of board performance and what happens in a turn, as well as a base for further development and skill acquisition.

stance

Stance includes overall body position, position on the board, and weight distribution.

Body position: This will vary slightly from SL to SG but, in general, a good athletic stance is a relaxed position with all joints flexed. Hands should be approximately shoulder width apart and slightly forward at the hips in the direction of travel. The back should be rounded or hunched to form a "C" position from the waist to the shoulders.

Position on the board: This depends on the type and width of board, the size of the rider and personal preference.

Stance angle: A good point of reference would be to align the toe and heel of the boot flush with the respective toe and heel edge of the board, the angles becoming steeper with narrower boards. Keep in mind that, as a general rule, most racers ride with two or three degrees less on their back foot. Stance width generally falls within 17.5 - 19.5 inches, with smaller riders using a narrower stance and larger riders a wider stance. The position of the stance on the board will be 1/2 inch ahead to 1/2 inch behind the center for SL and GS and center to one inch behind for SG.

Weight distribution: This will change through the different phases of the turn, with the weight being slightly ahead of center at the initiation of the turn and recentering at the completion.

TURN INITIATION

Turn Initiation begins by moving off a working inside edge, accomplished by a weight transfer. The weight transfer is achieved with the upper body in a centered position and allowing the knees and hip to move forward and down through the fall line.

e d g i n g

Edging is controlled by inclination and angulation.

Inclination: At the initiation of the turn, project your body down the fall line towards the inside of the new turn, in order to unload the effective edge in the previous turn and load up the new edge with pressure. Maintain a good athletic stance and resist the temptation to compress and release the pressure as the g-force builds through to the completion of the turn.

Angulation: Move both knees and hips in the direction of travel. Be sensitive to how much movement is required and try to minimize that movement to complete the turn.

t i m i n g a n d C O O R D I N a t i o n

Timing and coordination includes looking ahead to anticipate what's coming, and adapting to these changes, including shifts in terrain and rhythm, as well as fluidity from one turn to the next.

Looking ahead: Always look at least two turns down the hill. This helps you anticipate what's coming and keeps the momentum moving down the hill, not across.

Adaptation: This includes changes in the line of travel, such as in a rhythm change in the course. This can range from small offset, where the turn can be initiated later, to a large offset, where the turn initiation has to be set up more and initiated sooner. It also includes changes in terrain, such as flats to steeps, where the rider must move forward as the pitch steepens to ensure the weight distribution stays centered on the board.

Fluidity: Consistent movement during turns. One turn should flow into the next.

sLaLom tuRns

Slalom turns are quick, rhythmical and aggressive. The turns are initiated by a small movement upward and forward down the fall line, allowing a weight transfer to take place. A rolling sensation of the knees and body places the board on edge and steering commences. Energy is built up as a result of the steering and, when released, is absorbed in the ankle, knee and hip joints. The upper body remains quiet, in an open position, and the feet travel underneath, allowing the board to displace into a new line. As the board shifts to the outside of the turn, pressure and edge angles are applied dynamically by flexing and angulating the knees and hip (moving them in the direction of the turn). Pressure and edging are continued until completion of the turn.

Steering is an important component of all turns. It is the link between pivoting and edging. Pivoting maintains control in speed and radius, and will vary according to the level of rider and the difficulty of terrain.

sLaLom DRiLLs

The drills and exercises listed can also be incorporated into GS turns and vice versa for those listed in the next section on GS. The drills are a fun way to introduce racing skills or to correct specific problems the rider may be experiencing.

Even after mastering the basic skills, the drills and exercises learned can provide a good point of reference and help avoid bad boarding habits. They are also a good way to exercise and warm up for a day on the slopes.

spiess exeRcise

From a straight gliding position, flex your knees and ankles while keeping the arms forward. Initiate the turn with a dynamic extension (jump), pivoting the back foot across the line of travel. The back of the board should be weightless in the pivot stage. After landing on the new edge, repeat in the opposite direction. Legs work underneath the upper body, which faces the line of travel. Maintain consistent rhythm during the entire exercise.

Skills Emphasized:
- improved independent upper and lower body movement
- flexion/extension
- pivoting
- timing

thousand jumps

Perform quick, short jumps throughout a complete turn, especially at the beginning. Keep your body moving down the fall line in the direction of the turn. If you can't jump, you may not be centered.

Skills Emphasized:

- vertical balance
- flexion
- fore/aft balance
- hip/knee angulation

Looking ahead

Begin on easy terrain and progress to more difficult. Pick a point in the distance, approximately 20 turns down the hill, and keep that point in focus until the turns are complete. This teaches racers to look several gates ahead, which is very important to eventual line control and timing.

Skills Emphasized:

- looking ahead
- reaction time

Giant Slalom

Giant Slalom turns are large radius, rhythmical turns with flowing movement, linking one turn to the next. The body position is more dynamic than for Slalom. The initiation of the turn is similar to that of Slalom, but with a more subtle flexion/extension and a strong projection of the hips, knees and upper body into the direction of the turn. The upper body also follows the direction of travel more closely. Arms are kept open and slightly forward, to help maintain lateral balance. The lower body absorbs variation in terrain, while hip and knee angulation fine tunes and maintains a consistently progressive edge angle. The turn is completed by progressive edging and pressure, which is maintained by standing solidly and resisting the forces against the board. The balance between compression and leg extension controls the pressure on the board.

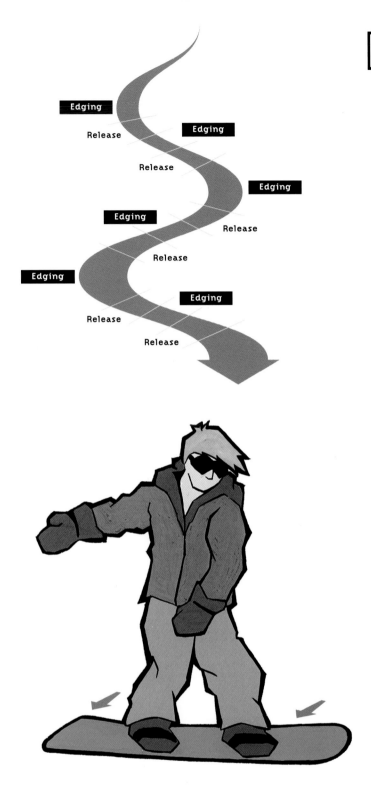

Edging

Release

Edging

Release

Edging

Edging

Release

Edging

Release

Edging

Release

Release

TURN INITIATION EXERCISE

Throughout the turn, project the hips, knees and upper body into the direction of the turn. Release immediately, so the board is running flat again, and repeat. Be aware of other people on the slopes as this exercise takes up a lot of room. This is a good exercise to develop the sensation of the body mechanics required to initiate a turn.

Skills Emphasized:

• vertical balance
• flexion (knees and hip)
• upper and lower body separation
• edge control
• turn initiation

HOCKEY STOP

From a straight, gliding position, use a dynamic motion to unweight the board. During that motion, shift your weight forward on the board to allow the back foot to pivot the board quickly around the front foot, across the line of travel. Recenter your weight on the board, and apply more edge gradually to stop. Repeat this exercise for both toe and heel side turns.

This exercise can be fine tuned to the point where the rider does not actually come to a stop. Instead, the rider pivots to a desired direction and speed, then applies edge pressure to continue in a carving turn across the hill. It is this type of control the rider ultimately wants to develop, to prepare for varied conditions and terrain.

Skills Emphasized:

• pivoting
• flexion/extension
• edge control
• speed control

ALL TERRAIN

Ride in a variety of snow conditions and terrain. Try moguls, steeps, flats, side hills, gullies etc. Round out and pivot the initial part of the turns more than usual in order to control your speed. All the basic skills apply, but everything should be more subtle, relaxed and centered in order to make it easier to absorb the bumps and stay balanced in rougher terrain. A more exaggerated flexion/extension may also be necessary to make the board weightless and pivot in the initial part of the turn.

Skills Emphasized:

• versatility
• balance
• adaptability
• flexion/extension
• edge control

gate training

Gate training has to be integrated gradually over a long enough period of time to allow for reinforcement of the basics learned outside the gates. Even at the height of the competitive season, the percentage of time a world cup-level rider spends in gates (maximum 75%) has to be balanced with time outside the gates (minimum 25%). The time spent in gates should be of a very high quality, and motivate the rider to further skill development and fine tuning outside the gates.

Entry-level gate training will promote rapid improvement both in and outside the gates. The largest improvements will come initially from expanding the rider's comfort zone to the point where getting around the gates becomes easy and the only hurdle is how to do it faster.

All the skills learned in the open slopes apply in a course. The big difference in a course is that the gates control the rider's path down the mountain. The fastest line down the hill is the most direct, with the least amount of pivot. This, however, is dictated by the terrain and the course, which will determine how early or late the turn initiation will be and, ultimately, the line through the course. Steeper terrain, a rougher course (ruts and bumps), and more offset turns all require earlier turn initiation, forcing the line to be more set up (rounder). Flatter terrain and less offset turns allow for later turn initiation and, therefore, a more direct line. Understanding a course and how to approach it takes years of experience, but the following basic line interpretation will be a good place to begin.

BASIC LINE INTERPRETATION

Giant Slalom (Steep Terrain)
$1/4$ of the turn is completed before the gates

Giant Slalom (Medium Terrain)
$1/2$ the turn is completed before the gate

Giant Slalom (Flat Terrain)
$2/3$ of the turn is completed below the gate

Slalom (Steep Terrain)
$2/3$ to $1/2$ of the turn above the gate –
dynamic flexion/extension

Slalom (Medium Terrain)
$1/2$ to $1/3$ of the turn is above the gate

Slalom (Flat Terrain)
$1/3$ to $1/4$ of the turn is above the gate –
less flexion/extension and quicker edge transfer

RHYTHM methods

The line will also change as the rhythm of the course changes and as the course deteriorates (ruts form) with more and more riders. Rhythm changes are generally used to follow the changes in the terrain, but they are also used to increase the technical difficulty and add variety to the course. The following are some examples of common rhythm changes:

SIDE HILL COMBINATIONS

turn RADIUS

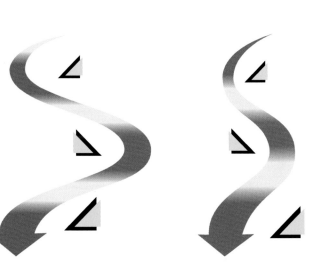

Giant Slalom
$^1/_2$ to $^3/_4$ of the turn is completed
before the gate

Slalom
$^2/_3$ of the turn is completed
below the gate

Large Offset
$^1/_2$ to $^3/_4$ of the turn is completed
before the gate

Small Offset
$^2/_3$ of the turn is completed
after the gate

DELAY/BANANA

This is a double-gate combination, used to achieve a drastic change in rhythm, bringing the rider from one side of the hill to the other in one big turn. Instead of the typical right-left movement around alternating gates, the gates will be set so that the rider will make one long turn around two gates in a row.

- $^1/_2$ to $^2/_3$ of the turn is completed before the gate
- $^1/_2$ of the turn is completed between the two gates
- $^1/_2$ to $^2/_3$ of the turn is completed after the gate

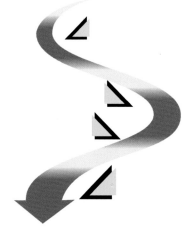

ROUGH AND RUTTED COURSE

As ruts develop in the course and it becomes rougher, the line will have to be set up more and the initiation of the turn will have to start earlier. No longer is the rider's path controlled just by the gates but also by the ruts. Trying to ride too tight in the line of the ruts will generally leave the rider fighting the steep bank created on the inside part of the rut, and having to edge harder than necessary to complete the turns. Instead, the rider should move the line out, thus riding through the flat part of the rut, where they can be more relaxed.

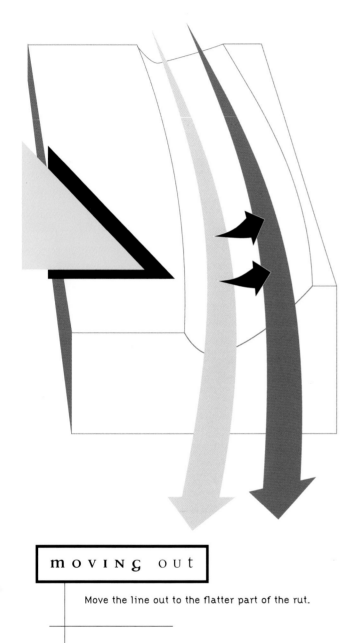

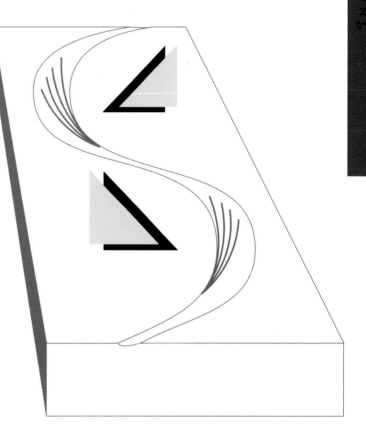

moving out

Move the line out to the flatter part of the rut.

pivot

Another trick as the course roughs up is to increase the pivot, turning the board across the line of travel before the gate, similar to setting up, but providing more control. This will also allow a more direct line into the gate.

Understanding and practicing these basic skills and drills is an excellent way to improve your racing ability. For those who seek faster improvement and to further establish these basics, a training program with a coach is recommended. These programs provide a good training atmosphere and a fun, social environment.

With or without a coach, learning to race is the hardest thing to do on a snowboard. At the end of the day, though, the rewards generated from a series of powerful, fast, clean carving turns through a course are worth the hard work, and can only be compared to the ultimate day in powder.

12

competitive

SNOWBOARDING

international snowboard federation (isf)

In 1991, the International Snowboard Federation (ISF) was founded to bring together snowboard clubs and associations from all over the world and act as a worldwide governing body. The winter of 1991/92 saw the first ISF World Pro Tour. The first official ISF World Championships were held in Ischgl, Austria, in 1992. More than 240 competitors from 20 nations participated.

The ISF now organizes the ISF Championships, the ISF World Tour, the ISF Boardercross World Tour, and the ISF Invitationals. These events take place in Europe, North America and Japan. To enter, competitors must be members of the Pro Snowboarders Association (PSA) and rated as one of the world's best snowboarders.

The ISF competitive disciplines are the Halfpipe, the Dual or Parallel Slalom, Giant Slalom, and the BoarderCross.

the HaLfpipe

Who can jump the highest, perform the most maneuvers in the air and land with grace wins the halfpipe. There are qualification rounds and final runs. Women start first, in the order of best to almost best on the current ISF World Rankings, and then the men, in the same order.

From the qualification rounds, the top eight women and 16 men enter the finals. Four judges score this event, looking for amplitude, precision of landing, balance, speed and variety. The judges' points are added together for the rider's total score.

the DUAL OR paRaLLeL sLaLom

Since snowboarding has a legacy of group riding and one-upmanship, Parallel Slalom is all about racing directly against an opponent. Two riders race each other down parallel 300 meters tracks through 25 gates with an average distance of 13 meters between each gate. There are two qualification runs and a knock-out final. As is the ISF tradition, women compete first and the best in the group lead the way. Obviously, the best time advances. Riders with the losing time receive a penalty. If they receive two penalties for poor time, they are out of the race.

the gIaNt sLaLom

The Giant Slalom is known as the speed discipline of snowboarding. True carvers enter this competition to race against the clock. The race track runs for 700 meters, with huge banked turns and naturally wide distance jumps, and a minimum of 25 gates with an average distance of 20 meters between each gate. Organized in two runs with the best women first and then the men, the top eight women and 16 men from the first run qualify for the second. A new course is set for the second run. The times of both runs are added together to determine the final ranking.

BOARDERCROSS ®

The youngest discipline of snowboard competition, BoarderCross gets its name from motocross racing. Freestylers and alpine racers ride together, at the same time, in heats of four. Designed with the goal of creating the greatest possible variety in terrain, it is divided into different sections, such as banked turns, jumps, rollers, tables and speed segments. Usually, six riders race simultaneously down the challenging course. Many view BoarderCross as the real snowboard discipline.

x-treme OR king-of-the-hill

Held at Valdez, Alaska, this competition brings together the best and craziest freeriders in search of the best all-round rider. The riders compete for three days. Day one is a sheer speed day – downhill for 2,000 to 3,000 feet of vertical, with five gates. Day two is slope style or obstacle course. Day three is Extreme. The rider must negotiate his or her way down steeps, open bowls and couloirs. The judging criteria are based on six things: fluidity, form, air, aggressiveness, and control. And staying alive. The judges sit at the bottom of the hill and watch the riders through binoculars.

13

tender loving care
Looking after your board

Remember, it is always a good idea to keep your board well maintained during the season in order to maximize its potential in the pipe or on the slopes. While you can do your own maintenance, it is a good idea to take your board to the store where it was bought, or to a shop specializing in snowboarding equipment, to have it tuned up. If you do decide to do your own maintenance, make certain you understand your board from nose to tail, as well as the equipment you'll be using. Here are the basic steps that should be followed when working on your board, courtesy of KUUSport MFG Ltd.

tuning

Well-tuned edges enhance performance greatly, provide better grip in icy conditions, improve speed control and reduce the risk of falling. Filing edges is a simple and quick procedure allowing a beginner to achieve professional results. Edges are generally sharpened square to the base, but modern technology has found that bevelling the edges makes snowboards turn easier and is recommended after flat filing or grinding.

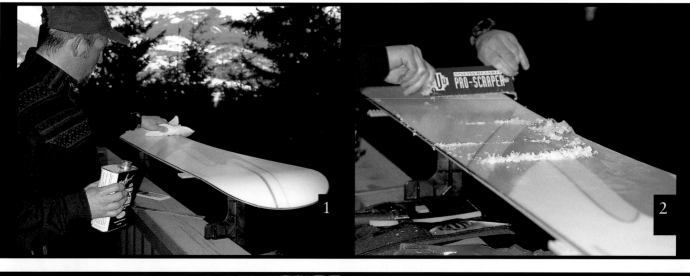

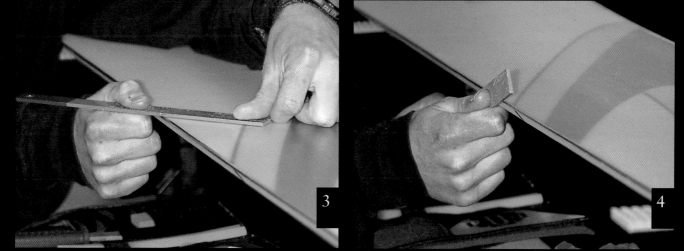

1 Use a true bar to examine the flatness of your base. Sight along the length of your base. If you see light at the center of the true bar, the base is concave, making it difficult to initiate a turn. If you see light at the edges, your base is convex, making the snowboard very unstable – the tip will wander from side to side. If the degree of convexity or concavity is severe, the snowboard must be tuned on a grinder.

2 Clean the base thoroughly using a wax remover

3 Fill gouges using a drip stick candle or base repair kit. Scrape down excess material using a stainless steel scraper.

4 If the base is slightly concave or convex, flat file to level. Run the file along the base using even strokes.

Hold the file at approximately a 45 degree angle to the edge and keep the file clean using a file card. Wipe the base regularly to avoid filings penetrating the base material.

5 Once the base is flat, use a pro file to bevel the base edge. Choose one of three angles: first, no sleeve (flat filed) for stable tracking; second, 1/2 degree for greater turning ability; and third, one degree for maximum glide and turning ability. Run the file at 45 degrees to the edge, using long even-pressured strokes. If the file won't cut on a section of the edge, rub the damaged section with a hard stone. Rub the damaged section vigorously until the file cuts evenly again. Continue until the entire edge is uniform.

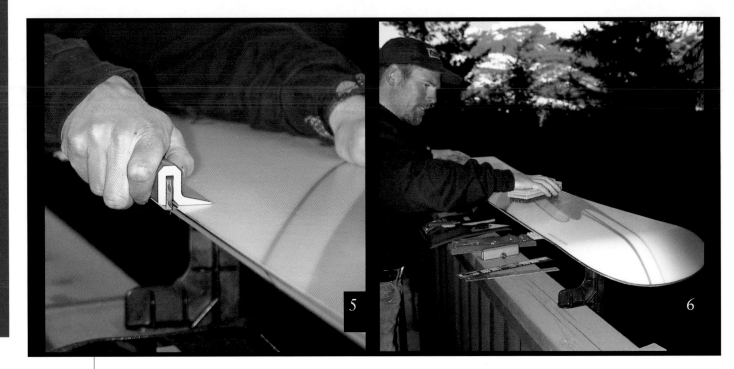

6   Using a 90 degree "ice buster" side edge sharpener,
    sharpen the side edges following the direction of the
    arrow on the file. Use continuous, long, even-pressured
    strokes until the side edge has a uniform finish. If a
    section of the edge is damaged, use a hard stone as
    in # 5 above. If riding in icy conditions, or to reach a
    higher degree of sharpness, use the 88 degree "ice
    buster", using the same procedure.

7   Dull the area of the edge that does not contact the
    snow using a gum stone. Run the gum stone evenly
    along both edges to remove any burrs.
8   Base edge filing requires only periodic maintenance
    when damage occurs. Side edge filing should be
    done regularly.

base repair

Damage at an edge or to the core material requires professional attention. To repair sintered base material, use a pro-fix base repair kit.
All work should be done prior to waxing and in a well ventilated area.

DRIP stick method

1   Concentrating on the damaged areas, clean the entire
    base with wax remover. Allow to dry for approximately
    ten minutes. Clean any material from the damaged area using
    the corner of a stainless steel scraper.
2   Light the candle and let it drip onto a stainless steel scraper.
    By keeping the lit end close to the scraper, you will achieve
    the proper blue flame. Rotate the candle and wipe any black
    carbon build up onto the scraper.
3   Fill in damaged areas to slightly above the base level. For
    deeper gouges make one pass, let cool, and repeat until
    material fills up to slightly above the base level.
4   With a stainless steel scraper, scrape to base level.
5   Use 220 grit base sanding paper to restructure the base.

SLICK stick method

1   Concentrating on the damaged areas, clean the entire base
    with wax remover.
2   Plug in a pro-fix base repair iron for 5 minutes.
3   Using the pro-fix base repair iron, melt a small amount
    of the repair slick stick into the damaged area. (The slick
    material is suitable for repairing all types of bases, including
    sintered bases.)
4   Smooth the melted material into the gouge, using the special
    tip on the pro-fix base repair iron.
5   Let repaired areas cool, then level with a stainless steel
    scraper. The sharper the scraper, the easier the excess
    material is removed.
6   For the final finish, use 220 grit base sanding paper or Tex pad.

Note: Repair slick stick turns brown if the repair iron gets too hot.
Unplug the iron and let cool, then resume work.

1

2

3

4

waxing INSTRUCTIONS

1 Clean the base thoroughly using a biocitron wax remover. Allow 10 minutes to dry.

2 Choose the appropriate base structure:
• Wet snow (criss-cross pattern). Use a stainless steel brush.
• Cold snow (straight line pattern). Use a brass brush.

3 Select the wax ideal for the conditions. If you are unsure, select a universal wax.

4 Using a professional waxing iron, press the bar at 90 degrees to the sole of the iron and let the molten wax drip evenly onto the base. Then in a back and forth motion, use the waxer to spread the wax, advancing when it has melted. If the wax begins to smoke, turn back the thermostat slightly. For best results, make

sure you have even penetration along the entire base. If the base is very dry, several coats may be necessary. When the entire base has an even coating of wax, allow to dry for approximately 20 minutes.

5 Scrape the excess wax off using a plexi scraper. Brush using a horsehair or nylon brush.

6 Structure the wax with a horsehair or nylon brush as in the base structure done prior to waxing. Do not polish the base after waxing.

That's it, the basics of board maintenance, from tip to tail. Once you've completed your repairs, made your adjustments and waxed your board, you're ready to hit the mountains once again. Good boarding!

180: A 180 degree spin on the snow or in the air.

360: The same as doing two 180 degree spins.

Angulation: Created by the lower body, i.e. hips, knees, and ankles, compensating for large edge angles by keeping the upper body balanced over the board's edge.

Axis: The central line around which your body spins during a rotation.

Backside: When your back faces the wall.

Balance: Think of your body as a skeletal structure. You are balanced when you are structurally aligned over your feet.

Base: The running surface of your board.

Base of support (BOS): Essentially, your feet.

Binding Positioning: You can adjust your bindings to match your riding style and daily snow conditions.

Bindings: Bindings are attached to the board with screws, and provide the interface between the boot and board.

Body angulation: Created from the board edge upward, involves your lower body and should be proportionate to the edge angle of the board, allowing the upper body to remain upright and centered over the board.

Bone: Refers to any time you straighten out your leg during an air (see Poke).

Camber: Camber is the arch in your board.

Cants: Small bevelled wedges under the boot which force the foot to lean.

Carving: A turn with no skid or slide, producing a clean rut in the snow.

Carving 360: Turning 360 degrees, carving a full circle in the snow as you turn.

Center of mass (COM): Think of it as just inside your navel.

Compress: Bend at the knees and ankles.

Couloirs: Narrow steep runs in between rock formations, calling for shorter radius turns.

Credit card air: Very small air.

Deck: The platform where people can watch riders perform their tricks along the pipe.

Down-unweighting: Flexing your knees and ankles and extending the legs out to the side, a lateral move.

Dual Slalom/Giant Slalom: May be run on courses resembling Slalom or Giant

Dynamic Carving Turns: Adding extension and flexion quickly in your carved turns.

Dynamic Sliding Turns: Adding extension and flexion quickly in your sliding turns.

Edge angle: The angle between the base of your board and the snow.

Edges: There are two types of edges, solid and cracked. A solid edge is continuous, wrapping around the entire board for added strength. The cracked edge is intentionally cracked in very small sections to offer more flexibility.

Edging: The act of putting the board "on edge." Controlled by inclination and angulation.

Effective Edge: The running length of your board.

Eurocarving: Inclining or banking into the hill so much that your arm and body touch the snow. This turn evolved from the European riders. With time you will be carving at high speed, scraping the surface of the snow and banking or leaning into the hill like an expert Eurocarver.

Extend: Stretching, as when snapping out of the turn.

Fakie: Riding your board backwards, one of the most important and fundamental skills of freestyle snowboarding.

Falling Leaf Sideslip: Controlling your direction by steering the board with your feet, moving back and forth like a falling leaf – hence the name.

Fall Line: The imaginary path a ball would follow if rolled down a hill.

Glossary

Flats: The level portion of a hill or mountain (no incline).

Flat: The floor of the pipe.

Flex: The stiffness or softness of your board.

Freecarver: An alpinist who wants performance and versatility .

Freerider: This rider takes advantage of the whole mountain, riding from top to bottom.

Freestyle boards: Designed for the halfpipe, the snowboard park or milking the mountain for hits.

Freestyle/Freeride: Used only with soft boots and usually has two straps, very versatile for freestyle and freeriding.

Frontside: Frontside is when you face the wall during a turn or air maneuver.

Garland: An exercise represented by a collection of incomplete turns. Once you can quickly and confidently put the board on edge, try to hold the edge longer, and, to avoid sliding, keep the pressure equal over both feet.

Giant Slalom: Run on two different courses marked with triangular panelled gates, over a faster, longer and more open line.

Giant Slalom Turns: Large radius, rhythmical turns with flowing movement, linking one turn to the next.

Goofy footed: Riding with your right foot forward.

Grabbed Airs: Derived from the world of skateboarding, where the rider grabs the board to hold it in place and stabilize it.

Green slope: A beginner's slope for the easiest run and terrain.

Handplant: When the rider gets inverted above the lip and supports his or her body weight with one hand.

Hardpack: Icy snow, packed solid by frequent riders or changes in temperature.

Inclination: Leaning or banking your body into the hill when you turn.

Indy Grab: Grabbing the board toe edge between your feet with your back hand.

Inserts: These are small threaded holes in the board for the bolts used to mount the bindings.

Inverted: Upside down.

Jet Turning: Using the tail of the board for sudden, powerful ends to turns by applying pressure to the board from tip to tail. A fluid move that should be left to the expert who has full understanding of stance and balance.

Jump turns: Pivoting turns while airborne. The only way to jump off the ground, whether on the flats or steeps, is to spring off your knees. A strong flexion and extension through the knees and ankles is required.

Leash: A safety device attached to the front binding and secured to your front leg when riding.

Lip: The top of the pipe wall.

Method Air: Kicking up your board behind you while grabbing heel side with your front hand.

Moguls: Bumpy terrain, requiring expert balance and very fast response.

Mute Air: Grabbing the board's toe edge with your front hand and doing a shifty sideways.

Nollie: Like an ollie, this time beginning with your board's tail and ending with the board's nose.

Nose: The front tip of the board.

Nose and Tail radius: This is the shape of the nose and tail of the board.

Nose roll: Rolling or spinning off the nose of your board.

Off piste: Anywhere off the groomed runs.

Ollies: A basic air in which you use your legs to pull the nose of your board up, followed by the waist and tail in one smooth motion.

Open slopes: Wide, clear sections of the mountain, great for large, wide turns.

Park: This designated snowboard-only area is fully loaded with jumps, berms, rollers, rails and other obstacles, some natural, but mostly man-made jumps.

Pieps: An avalanche transceiver.

Pivoting: The act of turning or steering the board.

Plate binding: Made for hard shell boots only. There is very little play in the binding, allowing for a quick edge-to-edge response.

Poke: Refers to any time you straighten out your leg during an air (see Bone).

Powder: Fresh, untracked snowfall, preferably very deep and thick.

Pressure: As you start to link turns, your speed will increase, producing pressure on your board and body.

Pumping: Using your legs to generate up and down momentum for bigger airs.

Racer: Seeks minimum movement for maximum reaction, always pushing the limits of speed.

Regular footed: Riding with your left foot forward.

Rotations: Any spin in the air. A true definition of a rotation in a pipe is a 360 or more.

Ruts: The grooves created by carving turns on a snowboard.

Shifty: Moving the upper and lower body in opposite directions during an air (see Bone).

Sidecut: The difference in width between the nose, waist and tail.

Sideslipping: Controlling the angle of your board's edge against a gradient, in order to move, slow down or speed up while your board is perpendicular to the fall line.

Sidewall: This holds the board together, protecting the side and the material inside the board.

Skate: Gliding your board across a flat using a motion similar to skateboarding.

Skid: A slight drag in the snow while turning or pivoting. Finish your turns and control your speed by adjusting the skid.

Slalom: An event requiring the execution of many quick and precise turns. It is run on two different courses marked by triangular panelled gates. The gates are set in varying combinations which test the rider's skill and strategy.

Slalom turns: Quick, rhythmical and aggressive.

Slarve: Part slide, part carve.

Speed: The more time your board spends in the fall line, the faster you will go.

Spin: A rotation while in the air.

Stance: How you position your body over your board. Includes overall body position, position on the board and weight distribution.

Stance angles: Due to binding placement, riding style and snow conditions, stance angles always vary.

Stance width: The distance between your feet.

Steeps: Significantly sloped sections of a mountain.

Step-in bindings: Combines the best of both hard and soft boots to produce a fantastic all-mountain freeriding boot binding.

Stiffy: Any grabbed air where you straighten both legs in front of you.

Stomp pad: A resting place for your back foot when out of its bindings.

Super Giant Slalom: A one-run event demanding courage and judgement as well as technical skills, characterized by large turns and changes in terrain.

Surface lifts: There are four main types – Rope tow, T-bar, Poma and Platter. The Poma and Platter refer to the type of pulley or handle used. Poma, Platter and rope tows accommodate one rider at a time. T-bars are for two.

Swing Weight: The ease with which the board swings is proportional to the swing weight or length of the board.

Tail: The back tip of the board, behind the back foot.

Tail roll: Rolling or spinning off the tail of your board.

The Eye: Perception skills. When you can judge speed and distance, it is easier to make the necessary and appropriate adjustments to adapt to changes in the terrain – and you will minimize your time walking the flats!

Torsional stiffness: Torsional stiffness refers to how much your snowboard resists twisting or bending when you put it on edge and apply pressure to it.

Torso: Your upper body.

Transition: Curved section between the floor and the walls.

Trees: Gladed area of the mountain.

Troughs: The ruts between the bumps or moguls.

Turn initiation: Begins by moving off a working inside edge, accomplished by a weight transfer.

Up-unweighting: A vertical move in which you extend through your knees and ankles to "unweight" the board of pressure.

Vertical (vert): The section of the wall perpendicular to the pipe floor.

Waist: The narrowest part of the board.

Wave: Similar to the Garland except larger, it allows you to experience a turn without changing edges. Hold the carve even longer. To benefit from the wave exercise, practice on wide open runs.

Wheelies: Just like a wheelie on a bicycle, but on your board.

Whoop de doos: Bumpy terrain.

If you're hoping to take the lessons learned in this book and apply them, you might want to find out more to make learning an even more enjoyable experience. Here are some addresses that might come in useful on your journey through the mountains:

- **Greg Daniells Adult & Summer Camp**
  32 Dawlish Drive
  Box 109, Site 7, R.R. 1
  Port McNicoll, ON
  Canada   L0K 1R0
  Telephone: 705 534 7913

- **Canadian Snowboard Federation**
  250 West Beaver Creek, Unit 1B
  Richmond Hill, ON
  Canada
  L4B I7C
  Telephone: 905 764 0922
  Fax: 905 764 6814

- **Canadian Association of Snowboard Instructors**
  774 Decarie Blvd., Suite 310
  St-Laurent, Quebec
  Canada
  H4L 3L5
  Telephone: 514 748 2648
  Fax: 514 748 2476

- **United States Amateur Snowboarding Association (USASA)**
  315 East Alcott Ave.
  Fergus Falls, MN
  USA 56537
  Telephone: 218 739 3843 / 800 404 9213
  Fax: 218 739 4842

- **United States Ski and Snowboarding Association (USSA)**
  P.O. Box 100
  Park City, UT
  USA 84060
  Telephone: 801 649 9090

- **British Snowboard Federation (BSA)**
  5 Cressex Road
  High Wycombe,
  Bucks
  HP12 5PG
  Telephone: 01494 462225

- **International Snowboard Federation (ISF) — American Services**
  P.O. Box 5688
  Snowmass Village, CO
  81615
  Telephone: 970 923 7669

- **International Snowboard Federation (ISF) Europe**
  A-6020 Innsbruck,
  Pradlerstrasse 21
  Austria
  Telephone: 43 512 342843